noodles

other idg cookbooks by paulette mitchell:

The 15-Minute Gourmet: Vegetarian

The 15-Minute Gourmet: Chicken

The 15-Minute Single Gourmet

The Complete Book of Dressings

The Complete Soy Cookbook

noodles

paulette mitchell

IDG
BOOKS
WORLDWIDE

AN INTERNATIONAL DATA GROUP COMPANY

Foster City, CA • Chicago, IL • Indianapolis, IN • New York, NY • Southlake, TX

IDG BOOKS WORLDWIDE, INC.
An International Data Group Company
919 E. Hillsdale Boulevard
Suite 400
Foster City, CA 94404

 The IDG Books Worldwide logo is a registered trademark under the exclusive license to IDG Books Worldwide, Inc., from International Data Group, Inc.

For general information on IDG Books Worldwide's books in the U.S., please call our Consumer Customer Service department at 800-762-2974. For reseller information, including discounts and premium sales, please call our Reseller Customer Service department at 800-434-3422.

Library of Congress Cataloging-in-Publication Data

Mitchell, Paulette.
      15-minute gourmet : noodles / Paulette Mitchell.
        p. cm. — (15-minute gourmet)
      Includes index.
      ISBN 0-02-862568-4 (alk. paper)
      1. Cookery (Pasta) 2. Noodles. 3. Quick and easy cookery.
   I. Title. II. Series.
TX809.N65M58 1999
641.8'22—dc21   99-38995
                                                          CIP

Manufactured in the United States of America
10 9 8 7 6 5 4 3 2 1
First Edition

Interior and cover design by Scott Meola
Cover photo by Nora Scarlett
Clock image © 1995 Chris Collins/The Stock Market
Silverware image © 1999 Photodisc
Cover photo: Mostaccioli with a Trio of Sweet Peppers (page 3)

To Grandma, my first cooking teacher, who passed on the legacy of family recipes and always brought more to the table than the creations from her kitchen.

acknowledgments

Heartfelt thanks to my friends, each of whom contributed to this book in a unique way:

Nancy Cameron, Denise Dobrzenski, Nathan Fong, Stephanie Grossman, Raghavan Iyer, Barb Kennedy, Fran Lebahn, Cynthia Myntti, Linda Platt, Connie Reider, Marcia Nakashima Rogers, Peggy Struble, Darryl Trones, and Carla Waldemar.

I am especially grateful to Jane Dystel, my agent, and to Jennifer Griffin and Linda Ingroia, my editors at Macmillan. Thanks, also, to production editor Helen Chin, designer Scott Meola, photographer Nora Scarlett, and food stylist Delores Custer and her assistants Lisa Homa and Judi Orlick.

contents

preface

EVEN BEFORE I COULD HOLD A FORK, I LOVED NOODLES,
especially the ones my Czechoslovakian grandmother carefully rolled and cut by hand. While visiting her, I was always
intrigued to watch as she dried the noodles on hand-
embroidered towels hung over the backs of her bright red
wooden kitchen chairs. In the days that followed, her tiny
kitchen would be filled with the enticing aromas of chicken
noodle soup, creamed chicken over noodles, and my
favorite—a simple toss of noodles and dried bread crumbs.

Thanks to Grandma, noodles became my favorite comfort food. Her patient instruction, combined with noodles' ease of preparation, led to early successes in the kitchen that bolstered my confidence as I developed my culinary skills. Later, as a cooking student, I was delighted to learn that almost every cuisine boasts a form of noodle and that noodles have been universally enjoyed across generations for centuries. I realized the mouthwatering possibilities were endless. That was, for me, the end of spaghetti topped with commercially prepared tomato sauce!

My passion continues to this day. Luckily, my son is a noodle lover, too. I began this project just as he entered the teenage phase of waking up taller every morning—and with an insatiable appetite. Even after dining on noodle dishes nearly every night throughout that year, they are still among our favorite meals.

The overwhelming response I receive when offering pasta or noodle cooking classes affirms our national love affair with noodles. They have become the food of choice for health-conscious consumers. Noodles fill the bill without demanding a high price in either calories or fat; their complex carbohydrates are our best source of energy. One cup of unadorned cooked noodles provides about 200 calories, derived from 42 grams of carbohydrates, 7 grams of protein, and just 1 gram of fat. During digestion, the complex carbohydrates cause our brains to release the chemical serotonin, which makes us feel happier and more relaxed after a meal. So noodles are a "good mood food." Maybe this is one of the reasons we look forward to noodle dinners!

The term "noodles" describes all types of noodles—Asian and Italian, dried and fresh. This is a food for all seasons. Served warm, at room temperature, or chilled, noodles provide the canvas for the robust flavors of summer produce; and in the cooler seasons, they warm us as a sublime comfort food. Noodles pair well with nearly any fresh vegetable, with chicken and seafood, and even with legumes;

seasonings and herbs easily lend multicultural diversity. And the dishes are as beautiful as they are delicious.

For those of us in a hurry, as most of us are, noodles represent the ultimate in convenience food, too; a satisfying noodle dish can be on the table sooner than heating a tasteless frozen dinner. Toppings and sauces are easily prepared in the 15 minutes (or less) it takes to cook the noodles. Not only Italian pastas but also Asian noodles are now available in supermarkets throughout the country, and "fusion" cooking has given us permission to use our imaginations when combining noodles and the elements of worldwide cuisines in unique ways. Most noodle recipes are one-dish meals, needing only the addition of a salad and bread.

Noodles are a good choice for both novices and experienced gourmet cooks. By varying the sauces, noodles adjust gracefully to any occasion, offering possibilities for satisfying a group of hungry teenage boys or for a fine-dining experience to delight your most discriminating guests. Asian noodles and Italian pastas have been elevated to gourmet status as chefs in trendy restaurants showcase them in imaginative, visually impressive, and sophisticated dishes. In some communities, "concept" restaurants are being developed around the humble noodle.

The 100-plus recipes I developed for this book came from many inspirations. Some represent trendy dishes I have enjoyed in both Asian and Italian restaurants; others are classics, pared down for 15-minute preparation. Traveling is always a source of ideas. While writing this book, I visited noodle factories and Asian noodle shops, wandered through outdoor markets in the Asian and Italian sectors in several large cities, and feasted on dozens of bowls of noodles. At home, out of the simple necessity to get a weeknight dinner on the table in a hurry, I sometimes looked to pantry staples and the odds and ends of vegetables in the refrigerator. Other times, my goal was to combine the unexpected. Some dishes were planned for an elegant, intimate dinner. And with buffet service in mind to allow time for me, the cook, to enjoy my guests at a large gathering, several dishes were designed for do-ahead, large-quantity preparation. Best of all, some of my favorite noodle recipes came from valued friends of varied backgrounds who shared family recipes with me.

The recipes that follow reflect my personal style of cooking and eating. The dishes provide generous servings, allowing them to serve as one-dish meals; or if you prefer, many can be served in smaller portions as side dishes. Some incorporate chicken and seafood; most are vegetarian. The recipes all allow for versatility, so don't hesitate to improvise. Add a protein source or substitute other vegetables. And, of course, feel free to use noodles or pastas other than those in the ingredient lists. With a variety of dried noodles, staples in your pantry, and fresh vegetables and herbs in your refrigerator, monotony is banished and every noodle dinner becomes a flavorful adventure.

I encourage you to expand your culinary repertoire. These recipes rely more on the imaginative use of fresh ingredients and Italian and Asian staples than on elaborate technique. So I guarantee your success even if you are a novice. It's true that we have less time to cook, at least not the laborious old-fashioned, day-in, day-out cooking that Grandma is remembered for. The good news is that in just 15 minutes a delicious noodle meal can be on the table. These dishes will be some of the best you've eaten, because they are made at home, from scratch, using the best ingredients available.

My dad often told me, "Use your noodle." He was right!

introduction

WHETHER YOU ARE SHOPPING AT AN ITALIAN MARKET,

an Asian market, or even your nearby supermarket, the number and types of noodles available may seem overwhelming. Here is some basic information to get you off to the right start.

Italian Pastas

Just a few decades ago, we spoke of spaghetti and meatballs, chicken noodle soup, or macaroni and cheese. Kids loved noodles; they were considered filling but not sophisticated. Pasta? We didn't even know the word.

According to statistics, Americans now eat about 26 pounds of Italian pasta per capita each year. Italians, of course, are the world champions, averaging 60 pounds of pasta a year for every man, woman, and child in the country. This averages to five pounds per month, at least one plate of pasta six out of seven days a week. And most of that pasta comes from a box.

Many people have the persistent notion that pasta, to be good, must be freshly made by hand. The fact is that *pasta secca* (dry pasta) is usually preferable to *pasta fresca* (freshly made), although both contain the same high-energy nutrition. Fresh pasta is actually harder to work with than dried pasta. Sometimes it is made from bread flour; if overcooked even slightly, it turns to goo in the cooking water.

Fresh pasta, available in many pasta shops and some supermarkets, has a short life span—only a day or two, if refrigerated. If you want to keep a package for a longer time, most varieties can be frozen for up to three months. Frozen fresh pasta can be cooked without thawing and will take only a minute or two longer. Regarding making your own pasta, in my opinion, there's no need to invest the time when so many top-quality pastas are readily available.

For greater convenience, more varieties of pasta are available in dried form. If you store unopened containers of dried pasta in your pantry, they will keep for up to a year. Once a package has been opened, what remains will keep well in an airtight container. I have a large supply of dried pastas in a variety of shapes on hand at all times. It's comforting to know that even if I don't have time to go to the supermarket, I can always make a satisfying dinner from pantry staples.

Generally, imported dried pastas are preferable to American pastas because they are made from hard durum wheat flour that has been finely ground into amber-colored granules called semolina. Semolina has a high gluten content and very little starch, which ensures the pasta will have body (providing it is not overcooked). Water is added to the semolina to form a paste or dough, which is extruded through dies to produce the required shape.

The best-made pastas are extruded through bronze dies rather than the Teflon kind, giving the surface of the pasta a microscopic roughness that helps the sauce to cling instead of sliding off. Top-quality pastas are slowly dried at low temperatures for as long as 30 hours for spaghetti and even longer for more complicated shapes. Lesser-quality pastas are dried very quickly, which reduces some of the aroma and flavor of the wheat, as well as some of its nutritional value. For a top-quality product, choose higher-priced dried pastas imported from Italy. An easy way to distinguish by appearance is that low drying temperatures result in pasta with a pale, creamy hue; the high temperatures used for quick drying begin to toast the wheat, creating uneven coloring, cracks, and an "off" flavor. My recipes call for dried pasta; if you choose to substitute fresh pasta in these recipes, keep in mind that 1 pound of dried pasta is equivalent to about $1^1/2$ pounds fresh.

In addition to basic pastas, both dried and fresh specialty pastas are now also commonly available. Sometimes egg is added, giving the pasta a warm yellow color and increasing its nutritional value. For the cholesterol-conscious, some egg pastas are made using the egg whites only, with yellow coloring added. Egg pastas have a more tender texture after cooking and are sweeter. Some pastas have colors added, such as spinach green, tomato-paste red, saffron yellow, beet pink, or even the purple-black of squid ink; these provide visual interest. Pasta creators have also moved to the next dimension: pastas with flavors blended into the pasta dough, such as pastas with the additions of garlic, cracked black pepper, chili peppers, sun-dried tomatoes, red bell peppers, herbs, mushrooms, or shrimp. Rather than depending on a sauce for flavor, these pastas themselves take center stage. Because flavored pasta does add a bit of confusion in choosing the appropriate sauce, I usually use these varieties for a simple toss of pasta with olive oil and freshly grated Parmesan cheese.

Other specialty pastas vary from the wheat-based Italian pastas in both texture and taste. They may be made from corn, millet, Jerusalem artichoke, quinoa, buckwheat, soy flour, potato, or sweet potato. These pastas provide options for those who choose not to eat wheat, and they may be substituted in my recipes. (Check the labeling; some may also contain wheat flour.)

By some estimates, the number of commercial pasta shapes available in Italy exceeds 400. An important thing to remember is that pasta shapes are interchangeable. If you can't find a particular type called for in a recipe, simply use a pasta of a similar size and shape. Some shapes serve purposes; for example, the fluted surfaces, described in Italian as "rigate," help sauces and cheese to adhere. In general, light, delicate sauces go best with smaller pastas and thinner strands. Chunky sauces are best served with sturdy pastas like rigatoni or penne. Shapes like penne and radiatore, which contain curves and crannies, trap the sauce and other ingredients.

Stuffed pastas, such as tortellini and ravioli, are available fresh, frozen, and dried. I do not use dried stuffed pastas, because I prefer to avoid the preservatives necessary to keep a perishable stuffing, like cheese, from spoiling at room temperature. It's worth a trip to a specialty pasta shop to buy some of the more exotic fresh varieties, such as pumpkin-stuffed tortellini, one of my favorites. These can be topped with a sauce or tossed with a pesto; but simply a drizzle of olive oil and a sprinkling of top-quality Parmesan or Romano cheese can turn stuffed pastas into a delicious meal.

Italians generally use pasta as a small first or side dish, often with only a drizzle of olive oil or melted butter, and with or without freshly grated cheese. Americans usually consider pasta to be an entrée. Accordingly, my recipes are designed to be served in entrée portions. That usually means 3 to 4 ounces of dried pasta per serving, taking into account that vegetables and often a protein source are included in the recipe. When thin strands, such as angel-hair pasta, are used, fewer ounces of pasta are necessary. That's because the thinner the pasta, the more strands to the pound and the more surface to cover; therefore, more sauce is required and less pasta. Using my entrée recipes as side dishes will provide about twice as many servings.

Judging the right amount of dried pasta to cook does not require a precise measurement. If I need 8 ounces of spaghetti, for example, I just guess at half of a one-pound package. Pasta "sizers" are nifty gadgets available at gourmet shops that will help you determine the correct amount of pasta strands to drop into the pot; 3 ounces is approximately a 3/4-inch bundle. For short-cut pastas, I have provided a cup measurement in addition to ounces.

For pasta experts, the method for cooking pasta is a serious matter. The ideal pasta pot should be taller than it is wide; it should accommodate 6 quarts of water. The bottom needs to be heavy so the pot will withstand high heat, will conduct heat evenly, and will not warp over time. Using a special pasta pot with a perforated strainer insert will make draining easier; these pots can be found in most gourmet shops and cookware departments.

When cooking the pasta, keep in mind that too little cooking water results in a gummy and overcooked product that may stick together or to the bottom of the pan. Ideally, every 4 ounces of pasta should cook in at least a quart of water, and more is even better. Start with cold water, use high heat, and put a lid on the pot to speed things up as the water comes to a boil. Dissolve 1 to 2 teaspoons of salt per quart of water after it comes to a boil. (It takes longer, if salt is added to water before it boils.) If using fresh pasta, add less salt since it absorbs salt more readily than dried pasta. Using coarse sea salt rather than table salt will enhance the flavor of the pasta without adding an overly salty taste (see Tip, page 73). Salt can be reduced if your sauce is salty or eliminated if you are concerned about your sodium intake; but be assured that if you do choose to salt the water, most of the sodium goes down the drain with the cooking water. When salt is omitted, remember that the added flavor will come only from the sauce. Adding oil to the water is not necessary to keep the pasta from sticking, providing that you use a large enough volume of cooking water.

While you are waiting for the water to come to a boil, assemble your equipment: You'll need a long-handled fork, tongs, or a wooden spoon for stirring the pasta when it starts to cook and to retrieve some later to test for doneness. Set a colander or a large strainer in the sink. This is also the time to assemble, measure, and begin chopping the other recipe ingredients.

The water must be at a full rolling boil before you add the pasta. When adding the pasta, stir to immerse it in the water and to prevent sticking. If you're using long strands of dried pasta, allow the immersed ends to soften before pushing the remainder under the water. It is not necessary to cover the pot; in fact, it is easier to check the pasta if the pot is uncovered. Allow the water to return to a full boil, then lower the heat slightly so that the pot doesn't overflow. Begin your timing.

The water should continue to roll gently as the pasta cooks; this constant temperature is easier to maintain with a large volume of water. The pasta will also cook more evenly, since the pasta will swirl around in the moving water. Stir the pasta occasionally to avoid clumps that will cook unevenly; with your spoon reach down to the bottom of the pot and around the sides to dislodge pieces that may be adhering. Be careful when stirring stuffed pastas so you don't tear the dough and release the filling.

Shape will determine how long the pasta must cook. Fine strands cook very quickly; heavy, thick shapes will require more time. Imported dried pastas often take a little longer than American-made pasta; the average cooking time is 8 to 10 minutes. Because fresh pasta is already moist, it cooks very quickly—some shapes in just seconds.

Overcooking is the single most common pasta failing; yet undercooked pasta will have an unpleasant starchy taste. For the most satisfying results, the cooked pasta should retain a pleasant, tender-but-firm, or slightly chewy, texture. The Italians call this delicious state *al dente*, which means "to the tooth." I have provided average cooking times for each pasta shape with my recipes, but use them only as suggestions. If I am using dried pasta, I set my kitchen timer for one minute less than the minimum suggested time; that's when I begin to test and taste. When you cut a strand of cooked spaghetti, it will appear cooked through, except for a tiny spot at the center of the strand; the Italians call this the *anima*, or the soul of the pasta. Testing shaped pastas means checking for doneness at the thickest point, such as at the pinch in the center of bow-tie pasta. Watch fresh pasta constantly as it cooks; fresh angel hair, for example, may need to cook for just 30 seconds.

When the pasta is done, trust your instincts; immediately dump it into the colander, keeping in mind that residual heat will cook it just a little more. Drain it well, shaking the colander gently. Rinsing the pasta is not necessary; this step just cools down the pasta. It also removes the starchy layer on the cooked pasta that helps the sauce to bind with it.

The exception is if you will be serving the pasta chilled. Then rinse it in cold water to stop the cooking process and drain the pasta again thoroughly. Do not let the pasta dry out; a little water clinging to the strands will help to keep the pasta moist. As it cools, pasta will continue to draw the surrounding liquid into itself; if the pasta is dry when the sauce is added, then it is the sauce that becomes absorbed.

For speed of service, many restaurant chefs partially cook the pasta ahead of time and remove it from the water just before it reaches the *al dente* stage; they then drain and cool the pasta. Just before serving, it is immersed into rapidly boiling water for 5 to 10 seconds, just long enough to reheat it. I do not recommend this for the home kitchen, except as a way to reheat unadorned leftover pasta.

If you follow my recipe instructions, your pasta and sauce should be done at nearly the same time. But if it's necessary to hold the cooked pasta for a few minutes, transfer the pasta from the colander to the still-warm but dry pasta pot. If you are concerned about the pasta sticking together, add a tablespoon or so of olive oil or canola oil (depending on the recipe), just enough to coat the pasta, and toss gently. Cover the pot until the pasta is ready to be sauced.

In addition to overcooking pasta, another problem may be oversaucing it. The Italians use a light coating of sauce so it doesn't mask the pasta's taste and texture. There should be sufficient sauce to lightly coat each strand of pasta—no puddles of oil or sauce in the bottom of the dish. A rule of thumb is that the sauce should complement rather than conceal the pasta; less sauce is usually better than more. For warm dishes, the other ingredients and sauce are added to the hot noodles. Often the pasta pot is rinsed with hot water; the drained pasta, sauce and other ingredients are put into the pot, and the combination is briefly tossed over medium heat to ensure that the dish is evenly heated for serving. To incorporate these ingredients into the pasta, toss gently using two large forks. Then serve the warm dish within minutes after saucing.

I have provided advance preparation information whenever applicable. For some warm pasta dishes, the sauce can be made in advance, refrigerated, and then reheated. Except for dishes meant to be served chilled or at room temperature, it is always best to cook the noodles and add the warm sauce just before serving. If there are leftovers, I generally reheat pasta dishes in the microwave.

The good news for 15-minute cooking is that simplicity and ease of approach are the keys to good Italian pasta. The best sauces are simple sauces. They're made with a limited number of ingredients, so the quality of each is very important. This means using fresh ingredients whenever possible—not just vegetables but herbs, too. Almost any supermarket carries all of the Italian pantry staples that you will need; the good stuff is worth the price. Key Italian ingredients are olive oil (extra-virgin is specified in uncooked recipes), aged balsamic vinegar, and real Parmesan cheese, ideally Parmigiano-Reggiano. I have provided Tips with the recipes to guide you in making the best ingredient selections.

Asian Noodles

After years of eating Italian pasta, I find Asian noodles an equally satisfying, and often more exotic, alternative. In Asian countries, noodles are a staple in everyday life; yet food there is much more than sustenance. Preparation, presentation, and ritual are as important as the taste; and eating is an experience that transcends the palate. To the experts, making noodles is an art form; and to most Asians, noodles have significance beyond their culinary and nutritional properties. They are traditionally served at New Year celebrations and in honor of birthdays. When a family member or friend is sick, visitors often bring a gift of noodles. The distinctive feature of all Chinese noodles is that, no matter what type, they are never made short. The long noodles are prized as a symbol of long life.

Most Americans can name dozens of Italian pastas without much effort. But although many people believe that pasta was invented in China before making its way around the world, Asian noodles are less familiar. If you visit an Asian market, the number of noodles is astounding. But that special trip may not be necessary. If you take a close look at the shelves in the Asian section of your favorite supermarket, you will be surprised at the number of noodles available. Even many bottled Asian recipe ingredients, such as hoisin sauce and plum sauce, can be found on supermarket shelves. Produce sections boast a sumptuous array of produce used in Asian cooking, including Chinese cabbage, bok choy, shiitake mushrooms, and snow peas. For a few of the bottled ingredients, you'll need to make an occasional trip to the Asian market; be assured that these products store well in your refrigerator.

Getting to know Asian noodles may be a challenge because of unfamiliar packages. Some noodles are sold in strands; others are formed into blocks. Adding to the challenge is the lack of standard labeling; one producer's "rice vermicelli" is another's "thin rice stick." Cooking times and methods also vary; one bag of rice stick noodles suggests a cooking time of two to three minutes, while another gives six to eight minutes. In developing the recipes for this book, I used commonly available dried Asian noodles from the supermarket whenever possible; the suggested cooking times are taken from those packages. But keep your eye on the noodles because you may be surprised by how quickly they cook. In each recipe, I have also provided an appearance test to guide you if you are using noodles from packages without instructions in English or if you buy fresh rather than dried noodles.

Dried Asian noodles will keep indefinitely if stored in an airtight container in your pantry. If you buy fresh noodles, plan to use them within two to three days; keep them tightly wrapped and stored in the refrigerator. This especially applies to the fresh noodles that have been coated with oil; storing them longer than a few days encourages rancidity, which spoils the taste and may create a health risk.

Just about all of the suggestions that apply to cooking Italian pastas apply to Asian noodles. Like their Italian cousins, Asian noodles require a generous amount of cooking water to prevent sticking. If you read the package ingredient lists, you'll find that many Asian noodles contain salt. For this reason and because salty ingredients—such as soy sauce and chili paste with garlic—are ingredients in many of the recipes, I do not add salt to the cooking water. After you add the noodles to the water and it returns to a boil, stir the noodles gently to separate; those that are packaged in blocks need to be separated with a fork as they cook.

Like Italian pastas, Asian noodles are best when they are not overcooked. Cooking times generally are shorter than those required for dried Italian pastas, making them ideal for 15-minute recipes. It's a good idea to begin tasting for doneness a couple of minutes before you think the noodles should be ready. Some Asian noodles, such as soba, taste best if they are just a touch past the *al dente* stage; when you taste them, you'll be able to recognize perfectly cooked noodles.

In some cases, rather than cooking in boiling water, some Asian noodles are simply soaked in hot or boiling water. In other recipes, the noodles are cooked and then rinsed under cold running water; then they are reheated later on the stove as they are combined with other ingredients, such as in the East Indian Noodles with Split Peas and Cashews (page 77). Both soaked and cooked noodles must be drained well but not allowed to dry out. Even though Asians like their noodles long, you may want to shorten them into manageable lengths to make them easier to eat; for example, I usually use kitchen shears to cut cellophane noodles after they have softened and before using them in recipes.

Although some cooks suggest that Asian noodles are interchangeable or that Italian pastas can be substituted, purists disagree. Each of the Asian noodles has distinct flavors and visual properties that are lost when substitutions are made. While Italian pastas are almost exclusively made with wheat flour, Asian noodles are much more diverse. They can be divided into three basic groups: wheat, rice, and a miscellaneous category that includes noodles made from beans. Although there are many types of Asian noodles, I'll describe only those that are used in the recipes in this book.

Asian wheat-flour noodles most closely resemble Italian pasta. Some are sold in long, straight strands (Chinese noodles); others are curly and tightly packed into a block (Japanese noodles). The noodles themselves may be round or flat. Some, such as Chinese egg noodles, are flavored by the addition of egg, giving them a yellow color. To confuse matters, some wheat-flour noodles are labeled "imitation egg noodles" or "imitation noodles," indicating that they are dyed to resemble egg noodles but actually contain no egg. Other wheat-flour noodles have flavorings added, such as shrimp, crab, or chicken.

- **Chinese lo mein noodles** are made with wheat flour and water or wheat flour and eggs; the flat strands are $1/8$-inch wide, or sometimes a bit wider. As an exception to the rule, linguine and spaghettini make satisfactory substitutes in some recipes.

- **Soba** are Japanese noodles made from a tradition that goes back more than 400 years. Originally they were made with buckwheat flour, water, and salt. Today regular wheat flour also is added; its gluten helps to hold the noodles together. These straight, flat, brown noodles remain a favorite in Japan, where they are meticulously prepared by soba masters. The noodles are valued because of their nutty flavor and high nutritional value, including protein, B vitamins, minerals, and dietary fiber. In Japan, soba are most often served cold with a spicy dipping sauce or hot in soups; but they lend themselves to warm dishes and salads as well. Here they are sold in many health-food stores, as well as in supermarkets.

- **Udon noodles** are white Japanese noodles made with wheat flour, water, and sea salt. They are typically round or flat, and they can be wide and thick or thin and delicate. Udon has a slippery texture after being cooked.

- **Ramen noodles** are made with wheat flour and salt. After these thin curly noodles are extruded, they are folded over and are dropped into a block-shaped mold. Most manufacturers then deep-fry the noodles in oil, which accounts for the oil listed in the ingredients. Some brands are baked rather than fried; this is indicated on the package label. Either can be used in my recipes calling for ramen; but because of the reduced fat and a flavor that I prefer, I recommend baked ramen noodles in my recipes. Ramen noodle packages come with a packet containing spices, dried foods, other flavoring agents, and preservatives. The intention is that the packet is to be used to flavor the broth in which the noodles are cooked, creating instant soup. I discard the packet and use only the noodles in my recipes. The noodles of any particular brand are identical, no matter which flavor packet accompanies them. Because they are precooked, ramen noodles hydrate quickly when added to hot liquids; in fact, by the time the pad has broken apart, the noodles may be done. And because they are precooked, they can be crumbled and eaten crispy without additional cooking, as in Crunchy Sweet-Sour Ramen-Cabbage Salad (page 178).

Rice noodles are made with rice flour and water; sometimes salt is added. They contain no wheat flour so they are a good choice for anyone who is allergic to wheat; but because there is no gluten in rice, the noodles don't hold their shape as well as those made from wheat flour. Rice noodles can be recognized by their translucence and white-gray color; the shape can be either round or flat. The term "rice stick" applies to thin noodles, also called rice vermicelli; others are thicker and shaped like spaghetti. Other rice noodles include the wider, fettucine-like rice-stick noodles that are used in Southeast Asian cooking. Like ramen, these noodles sometimes are packaged with a flavoring packet; again I discard the packet and use only the noodles. It is especially important to keep dried rice noodles away from moisture when stored. Fresh rice noodles are found in most Asian markets either in the refrigerator or freezer sections; like other fresh noodles, they cook quickly, often requiring just 30 seconds in boiling water to soften them. After cooking, both dried or fresh rice noodles tend to clump together as they cool; often they are dipped in cold water to separate the noodles before adding them to a dish. The oil and sauces keep the noodles separate in completed dishes. Because rice noodles continue to absorb the liquid in recipes, refrigerating leftovers to reheat later is usually unacceptable.

Cellophane noodles, also called bean thread noodles, glass noodles, or sai fun, are made with the starch of mung beans, which we know best as bean sprouts, and water. Some also have potato starch, pea starch, tapioca, or arrowroot added. These, too, are a good choice for the wheat-intolerant. These noodles are coiled before being packaged in plastic; they are very brittle and have a cellophane-like translucence. They will keep indefinitely when stored in an airtight container. After being softened, cellophane noodles become almost transparent. They are virtually flavorless and hungrily soak up other flavors, so they are a natural medium for adding spiciness to a dish. For 15-minute recipes, choose thin cellophane noodles that can be softened by soaking in hot water for 8 to 10 minutes. Thick cellophane noodles may need to be plunged in boiling water and cooked until tender. Cellophane noodles also may be taken directly from the package and deep-fried in oil to make crisp noodle nests.

The Noodles

Here is an overview of the Italian pastas and Asian noodles called for in the recipes in this book.

ITALIAN PASTAS

These pastas are divided into categories by shape; you'll also find an explanation of the Italian name and a brief description. When making a recipe ingredient substitution, it often works best to select another pasta within the same shape category. But don't be limited by the shapes in this list; the multitudes of others that are available in supermarkets and Italian markets offer many other possibilities.

String Shapes

Thin solid strings

capellini: "angel hair" pasta; delicate and extremely thin strands

vermicelli: Italian for "little worms"; thin strands but thicker than capellini

spaghettini: very thin spaghetti, thicker than capellini and vermicelli

Medium solid strings

spaghetti: Italian for "a length of string or cord"

Flat strings

linguine: Italian for "little tongues"; flat strings about $1/8$-inch wide

Curly strings

long fusilli: Italian for "twists"; looks like spiraled spaghetti

Short strings

ready-cut spaghetti: spaghetti cut into pieces about $3/4$-inch long

Tubular shapes

Straight-edged medium tubes

rigatoni: short grooved tubes of macaroni about $1/2$-inch long

Bent short tubes

elbow macaroni: short curved tubes about 3/4-inch long

Tubular shapes(continued)

Diagonal-cut medium tubes

mostaccioli: Italian for "small moustaches"; about 2-inch-long tubes

penne: Italian for "pens," "feathers," or "quills"; similar to mostaccioli, about $1^1/2$ inches long

penne rigate: penne covered with small ridges

Long thin tubes with flat-cut ends

ziti: means "bridgegroom"; looks like long thin tubes of macaroni, about $1^1/4$ inches long

Short and curly shapes

Solid twists

rotelle: small round pasta that resembles a wheel with spokes, $1/2$ to 1 inch in diameter

rotini: spaghetti spirals about $1^1/2$ inches long

rainbow rotini: rotini tinted with vegetable coloring, such as spinach green and tomato-paste red

Ribbon shapes

Long ribbons

fettucine: Italian for "small ribbon"; noodles $3/16$-inch to $1/2$-inch wide

spinach fettucine: fettucine with spinach green coloring added

Short ribbons

spinach ribbon noodles: noodles tinted with spinach green coloring, about 2 inches long

Broad ribbons

mafalda: mini lasagna; $3/4$-inch wide ribbons with ruffled edges, about 1-inch long

Egg noodles

fine egg noodles: very thin noodles about $1^1/2$ inches long

spinach egg noodles: egg noodles tinted with spinach green coloring, about 2 inches long

wide egg noodles: $1/2$-inch wide by 2-inch-long egg noodles

medium egg noodles: $1/4$-inch-wide by 2-inch-long egg noodles

wide yolk-free egg noodles: egg noodles made with egg whites and no yolks

Shell shapes

pasta shells: $1/2$-to 1-inch-long sea shells

conchiglie: very tiny shells, up to $1/2$-inch long

Fancy shapes

alphabets: $1/4$-inch-tall letters

creste di gallo: ornate curved pasta shaped like a cock's crest, about $1^1/4$ inches long

farfalle: Italian for "butterflies," bow tie-shaped pasta about $1^1/2$ inches long

radiatore: Italian for "little radiators"; resembles tiny radiators with rippled edges, about $3/4$-inch long

rotelline: tiny (up to $1/2$-inch in diameter) round pasta that resembles a wheel with spokes

Short and curly shapes (continued)

Filled pillows (select fresh rather than dried)

ravioli: $1^1/_2$-inch square, round, or triangular-shaped noodles filled with cheese, meat, or vegetables

tortellini: $3/_4$-inch pasta stuffed with various fillings, then folded over and shaped into a ring or hat shape (larger-sized shapes are called tortelloni)

Others

gnocchi with potato: Italian for "dumplings"; $3/_4$-inch by $1^3/_4$-inch pieces

riso: tiny rice-shaped pasta, similar to orzo

ASIAN NOODLES

These noodles are divided into groups according to their primary ingredient.

Further details are provided on pages xxi to xxvi.

Wheat-flour noodles

baked ramen noodles: thin, curly noodles formed into blocks

thin Chinese wheat-flour noodles: long, straight thin strands

Chinese lo mein noodles: flat strands about $1/_8$-inch wide or slightly wider

Japanese noodles: curly noodles, tightly packed into a block

Chinese egg noodles: strands with the addition of egg to give them a yellow color

imitation egg noodles: strands dyed to resemble egg noodles but contain no egg

udon: white Japanese noodles, round or flat, thick or thin

soba: flat, brown straight Japanese noodles made with buckwheat flour

Rice noodles*

flat rice noodles: available in various widths

round rice noodles: available in various thicknesses

sometimes called rice sticks or rice vermicelli

Cellophane noodles

thin round cellophane noodles. Also called bean thread noodles, glass noodles, or sai fun; made with the starch of mung beans.

Using the Recipes

EQUIPMENT FOR 15-MINUTE NOODLES

As you read the recipes, you will find that very little equipment is necessary for getting your Italian pasta and Asian noodle creations on the table in a hurry. The basics are a set of sharp knives and a cutting board, a large pot, a colander, and serving dishes. In addition to kitchen basics, the list below takes into account utensils and equipment particular to pasta and noodle cooking and serving. I believe that high quality tools will enhance your cooking experience. Always buy the best you can afford and care for them meticulously.

- food processor
- large (12-inch) nonstick skillet
- large (5-quart) nonstick sauté pan with a tight-fitting lid—has straight deep sides allowing it to accommodate more liquid than a skillet with sloped sides
- stovetop grill pan (12-inch, preferably nonstick); (see Tip, page 7)
- garlic press
- cheese grater
- pepper mill
- slotted spoon
- hinged salad tongs
- pasta serving forks (pasta claws)

THE WELL-STOCKED PANTRY

In addition to many shapes and sizes of dried Italian pastas and Asian noodles and fresh vegetables and herbs, a well-stocked kitchen should contain some staples that are used in numerous recipes in this book. Page numbers refer to tips where you can find information on each ingredient.

- olive oil and extra-virgin olive oil—page 105

- canola or safflower oil—page 105

- flavored oils: roasted peanut oil, walnut oil, dark sesame oil—pages 112, 144, and 71

- vinegars: balsamic vinegar, red wine vinegar, white wine vinegar, rice vinegar, and rice wine vinegar—pages 148 and 146

- garlic—page 125

- fresh ginger—page 95

- onions—page 17

- shallots—page 23

- fat-free low-sodium chicken broth: in cans and in aseptic packaging—page 188

- vegetable stock powder—page 188

- canned tomatoes—page 29

- frozen vegetables: peas and corn—page xxxiii

- oil-packed sun-dried tomatoes—page 109

- Kalamata olives—page 122

- capers—page 142

- low-sodium soy sauce—page 183

- chili paste with garlic—page 89

- hoisin sauce—page 59

- whole peppercorns—page 110

- ground white pepper—page 93

- red pepper flakes—page 167

- coarse sea salt—page 73

Tips for 15-Minute Success

- Choose the freshest, best-quality ingredients.

- Read the recipe all the way through before beginning.

- Set out all of the ingredients and equipment before you begin.

- Organization is important for 15-minute success, so follow the sequence of steps numbered as described. Always begin by bringing a pot of water to a boil. Noodles that require a lengthy cooking time are added to the pot of water as soon as it comes to a boil; the sauce is prepared as the noodles cook. The noodles are also cooked first when they require cooling time before adding a sauce or dressing. Quick-cooking noodles to be served warm are added to the boiling water near the end of the 15-minute preparation time; the sauce preparation will be nearly completed. This coordination ensures that your pasta will be done when the sauce is ready to serve.

- Remember that efficient cooking does not follow a linear progression. To complete the recipes in 15 minutes, proceed through the steps without stopping. You will often be doing two or even three things at once, such as mixing an uncooked sauce or dressing while the vegetables and noodles are cooking. As you become accustomed to 15-minute cooking, this "kitchen choreography" will become second nature to you.

- Use a food processor for some procedures, such as shredding carrots or chopping onions. For hand chopping, use a sharp knife and an efficient, safe chopping technique.

- Use nonstick cookware to make dishes more healthful and to speed up cleanup. The amount of oil in my recipes is based on the use of nonstick cookware.

- Choose fresh vegetables unless otherwise specified. Frozen corn and peas are acceptable and are more practical than fresh for 15-minute recipes.

- Use fresh herbs whenever possible; quantities for dried herbs are provided only when their use is an acceptable alternative. Some herbs, such as cilantro, mint, and flat-leaf parsley, are never acceptable in their dried forms. Fresh or dried herbs often need to be added at different times in the cooking process, as noted in the recipe procedures.

- Determine cooking times by appearances as described; times are approximate and may vary by pan type and weight, the use of a gas or electric stove, differences in microwaves, etc.

- Advance preparation tips are included whenever applicable.

  - Sometimes a sauce or dressing can be made in advance to be tossed with hot freshly cooked pasta just before serving.

  - Because pasta is porous and will continue to absorb flavors, liquid and oil from sauces, the texture of noodles may become mushy. If you are not serving a dish just after it is prepared, often it is better to refrigerate cooked pasta separately from the sauce.

  - Plain cooked noodles will keep in an airtight container for up to 3 days.

- Variations are suggestions for alternative ingredients but don't feel limited by them. It is nearly always acceptable to use your favorite in-season produce or odds and ends of vegetables you may have on hand. You can often add seafood, chicken, pork, or beef to vegetarian recipes; or add more vegetables, omitting the nonvegetarian ingredients. Keep in mind that variations may take longer to prepare and will alter the nutritional values.

- Use pasta shapes other than those specified.

- Read the Tips for ingredient explanations. These may be helpful in knowing how to select or store some of the less-common ingredients and how to perform some basic procedures, such as toasting nuts or seeds. Refer to page references in the Index.

- Adjust seasonings, especially salt, pepper, and those that add hotness, according to your personal taste. These ingredients are listed as "or to taste." Take into account your tolerance for hotness and also that of your guests. You can also personalize the flavors by adding more or less of other items, such as garlic or cilantro. Sometimes the necessary amount of an ingredient is affected by the garnish you plan to use; for example, Parmesan or feta cheese will add saltiness.

- Each recipe includes a nutritional analysis per serving, based on the stated number of servings that the recipe yields. The ingredients have been analyzed in the form as listed, such as "low-sodium soy sauce" and "fat-free, low-sodium chicken broth." Dressings and sauces are included. Garnishes and variations will alter the figures.

- Feel free to double the recipes; most of them multiply well. As a rule of thumb, when doubling a recipe multiply the herbs times $1^1/2$, then add more to taste. The same is true for the ingredients adding hotness; for example, doubling the amount of chilies or red pepper flakes might make the sauce too spicy.

- As I tell my cooking class students, no one needs to know you spent only 15 minutes making dinner. Garnish your creations, serve your Italian pastas and Asian noodles with style, and present them with pride.

chapter 1

Warm Noodles

THESE 15-MINUTE ENTRÉES CELEBRATE THE CUISINES of many nations. You'll discover some novel combinations and a touch of fusion here and there. After all, Mexican chiles and black beans can be at home tossed with Italian penne. And Thai Coconut-Peanut Sauce (page 74) is delicious with lo mein noodles. But tradition has not been totally abandoned; you will also find pared-down versions of classics such as Pad Thai (page 68) and Linguine with Red Clam Sauce (page 8).

Most heated pasta and noodle dishes are at their best served really hot. Ideally, bring uncooked vegetables to room temperature before preparing the recipe; adding chilled ingredients will lower the temperature of hot noodles in a hurry. For most recipes, I suggest tossing the just-cooked noodles with the hot sauce over medium heat, just until the mixture is heated through. (You can use the pasta cooking pot; rinse it with hot water before adding the drained noodles and sauce.) Then it is important to serve the dish right away. Even if you have made the sauce in advance, it is always best to reheat it and then toss the sauce with hot, freshly cooked noodles.

I usually serve my warm Italian pasta and Asian noodle dishes in individual shallow pasta bowls; sometimes I spread the creations on colorful plates. For serving large groups, I use a large serving bowl and let guests help themselves.

Heated bowls retain the heat longer. This requires a little advance planning, but the flavor-enhancing touch requires only seconds of extra time. Use your choice of method: Preheat the oven to 350°F for about 15 minutes before dinnertime, turn off the heat, and place the dishes there until they are needed. Or fill them with hot water, let stand for a minute or two, and then dry each plate before filling with pasta. You can even drain the boiling pasta cooking water into the bowls, then rinse with hot tap water and dry before using.

For the feast to be complete, all you need to add is your favorite wine, some warm, crusty bread, and a salad. For a one-dish meal, I sometimes serve the salad on the same plate with the noodles by arranging the noodles atop a bed of greens, such as coarsely shredded romaine lettuce; the contrast of colors, temperatures, and textures is often appealing. Top off the meal with fresh fruit or another light dessert.

Keep in mind, too, that in smaller portions, many of these dishes can be served as first courses or as side dishes to accompany seafood, poultry, or meat.

mostaccioli with a trio of sweet peppers

Makes 4 servings

The sweetness of bell peppers is the flavor we're celebrating in this colorful dish. Stir strips of grilled chicken breast into the topping to make the dish more filling. Add a dash of red pepper flakes to make the flavor not only sweet but also zesty.

12 ounces mostaccioli (about 4 cups)

2 tablespoons olive oil, divided

1 small red onion, cut into $1/4$-inch-wide strips (about 1 cup)

1 red bell pepper, cut into 2-inch-long by $1/4$-inch-wide strips; about $1^1/2$ cups (see Tip)

1 yellow bell pepper, cut into 2-inch-long by $1/4$-inch-wide strips (about $1^1/2$ cups)

1 green bell pepper, cut into 2-inch-long by $1/4$-inch-wide strips (about $1^1/2$ cups)

2 teaspoons minced garlic

$1/4$ cup toasted pine nuts

$1/4$ teaspoon pepper, or to taste

Dash of salt, or to taste

$1/2$ cup fresh basil chiffonade (see Tip)

GARNISH (OPTIONAL)   freshly ground black pepper, freshly grated Parmesan cheese or chèvre cheese

1. Bring a large pot of water to a boil over high heat; add salt, then the mostaccioli. When the water returns to a boil, stir occasionally to separate the mostaccioli. Reduce the heat to medium-high and cook for about 12 to 14 minutes, or according to package instructions, until noodles are *al dente*.

2. Meanwhile, heat 1 tablespoon of the oil in a large nonstick sauté pan over medium high heat. Add the onion; cook, stirring occasionally, for about 3 minutes or until crisp-tender. Add the bell peppers and garlic; continue to cook, stirring occasionally, for about 8 minutes or until the bell peppers are tender. Stir in the pine nuts, pepper, and salt. Adjust the seasonings to taste. Remove from the heat and cover to keep warm.

3. When the mostaccioli is done, drain well; return to the pot. Add the remaining 1 tablespoon of oil and toss. Add the basil and toss again.

4. To serve, spoon the mostaccioli into pasta bowls; top with the bell pepper mixture.

PER SERVING: Cal 479/Prot 12.9g/Carb 74.2g/Fat 14.5g/Chol 0mg/Sod 44mg

Variation

- Stir a few tablespoons of Roasted Red Pepper-Walnut Pesto (page 111) into the cooked bell pepper mixture.

TIPS

- Bell peppers are most often sold in the mature green stage, fully developed but not ripe. Red bell peppers are vine-ripened green peppers, which are sweeter because they have ripened longer. Bell peppers are also available in gold, orange, and purple, all mildly flavored. Choose bell peppers that are plump, firm, and crisp, with no wrinkling or soft spots. Store in plastic bags in the refrigerator for up to 1 week.

- Large-leafed herbs, such as basil, and vegetable leaves, such as spinach and lettuce, may be cut into coarse shreds, called a chiffonade. Stack the leaves on a cutting board and roll the pile tightly. Slice across the roll to make fine or coarse strips, depending on the leaf you are using.

Mostaccioli with a Trio of Sweet Peppers (page 3)

herbed vegetables on capellini

Makes 4 servings

A fragrant mix of fresh herbs is a must for this dish, making it ideal for summertime entertaining. To complete the menu, brush chicken breasts, tuna steaks, or salmon steaks with olive oil; grill them and then sprinkle with salt and pepper. Place atop the capellini and top with the vegetables.

1/4 cup + 1 tablespoon olive oil

2 tablespoons fresh lemon juice

2 teaspoons minced garlic

1 teaspoon minced fresh thyme

1 teaspoon minced fresh oregano

1 teaspoon minced fresh rosemary

1/2 teaspoon pepper, or to taste

1/8 teaspoon salt, or to taste

6 ounces portobello mushrooms, cut into 1/2-inch-thick slices (see Tip)

1 red bell pepper, cut into 1/4-inch-wide lengthwise strips

8 asparagus spears, cut into 2-inch-long pieces

1 medium onion, cut into 1/4-inch-thick slices (about 1 1/2 cups)

12 ounces capellini (angel hair pasta)

GARNISH (OPTIONAL)   freshly ground black pepper; freshly grated Parmesan cheese, crumbled feta cheese, or chèvre cheese; sprigs of fresh thyme, oregano, or rosemary

1. Bring a large pot of water to a boil over high heat.

2. Meanwhile, in a large bowl, stir together 1/4 cup of the olive oil, lemon juice, garlic, thyme, oregano, rosemary, pepper, and salt. Add the vegetables and toss.

3. Heat a large skillet over high heat. Add the vegetables with the oil–lemon juice mixture and cook, stirring often, for about 4 to 6 minutes or until the asparagus is crisp-tender and all the vegetables are lightly charred in spots. Remove the pan from the heat; adjust the seasonings to taste.

4. When the vegetables are nearly done, add salt, then the capellini to the pot of boiling water. When the water returns to a boil, stir occasionally to separate the capellini. Reduce the heat to medium-high and cook for about 3 to 4 minutes, or according to package instructions, until noodles are *al dente*. Drain well; return the capellini to the pot and toss with the remaining 1 tablespoon of oil.

5. To serve, transfer the capellini to pasta bowls; top with the cooked vegetables.

> **PER SERVING:** Cal 527/Prot 14.1g/Carb 75.2g/Fat 18.9g/Chol 0mg/Sod 73mg

Variations

- Add other vegetables, such as yellow squash or zucchini, diagonally cut into 1/4-inch-thick slices.

- Cook the vegetables on a stovetop grill pan (see Tip).

- Before removing the vegetables from the pan, stir in a cubed tomato and/or about 1/4 cup sliced Kalamata olives.

TIPS

- Portobello mushrooms are large, dark brown mushrooms with an open, flat cap; the tops can easily measure 6 inches in diameter. Because of a long growing cycle, the portobello's gills are fully exposed, which means that some of the moisture has evaporated; this concentrates and enriches their flavor and creates a dense, meaty texture. Portobellos can be found in many supermarkets and in gourmet produce markets.

- Stovetop grill pans are available made from a variety of materials (some are nonstick, which I recommend); and they come in a range of shapes, sizes, and prices. What they have in common is raised ridges on the cooking surface that give foods cooked on the pan visually appealing grill lines along with a smokey, grilled flavor achieved quickly with little or no added fat.

linguine
^{with} red clam sauce

Makes 4 servings

Because clams, even those from cans, will toughen if overcooked, add them near the end of the cooking period and heat gently.

8 ounces linguine

Red Clam Sauce

1 tablespoon olive oil

2 teaspoons minced garlic

1 (28-ounce) can Italian tomatoes with
juice; coarsely chop tomatoes

2 tablespoons coarsely chopped fresh
flat-leaf parsley (see Tip)

$1/8$ teaspoon red pepper flakes, or to taste

Dash of pepper, or to taste

Dash of salt, or to taste

1 (6-ounce) can chopped clams, drained
($1/2$ cup clam juice reserved)

GARNISH (OPTIONAL)   freshly ground black pepper, freshly grated Parmesan cheese

1. Bring a large pot of water to a boil over high heat; add salt, then the linguine. When the water returns to a boil, stir occasionally to separate the noodles. Reduce the heat to medium-high and cook for about 10 to 12 minutes, or according to package instructions, until noodles are *al dente.*

2. Meanwhile, heat the oil in a large nonstick skillet over medium-high heat. Add the garlic; cook, stirring constantly, for about 1 minute or until fragrant. Stir in the tomatoes with juice, parsley, red pepper flakes, pepper, salt, and the reserved clam juice. Cook, uncovered, stirring occasionally, for about 6 minutes or until the sauce is slightly

thickened. Reduce the heat to low. Add the clams and stir gently for about 2 minutes or until heated.

3. When the linguine is done, drain well; return to the pot. Add the clam sauce and toss over medium heat just until heated through. Adjust the seasonings to taste.

PER SERVING: Cal 312/Prot 12.7g/Carb 53.2g/Fat 5.4g/Chol 27mg/Sod 380mg

ADVANCE PREPARATION   Covered and refrigerated, the sauce will keep for up to 1 day. Reheat gently and serve over hot, freshly cooked pasta.

TIP

Flat-leaf parsley, also called Italian parsley, has a more pungent flavor than the more common curly-leaf parsley. Wash fresh parsley, shake off the excess moisture, and wrap first in paper towels, then in a plastic bag. Refrigerate for up to 1 week. Stay away from dried parsley, which has little of the distinctive parsley flavor.

radiatore with
yukon gold potatoes
and spinach

Makes 4 servings

When I first ordered the pasta-potato combination in an Italian restaurant, I was pleasantly surprised at the compatibility of these two comfort foods. Here the potatoes, which can be cooked right along with the pasta, come to life with the addition of generous amounts of garlic and red pepper flakes.

12 ounces radiatore (about 4 cups)

2 medium or 1 large yukon gold potato, peeled and cut into 1-inch cubes (about 3 cups); (see Tip)

2 tablespoons olive oil

1 small onion, cut into $1/4$-inch-wide strips (about 1 cup)

2 teaspoons minced garlic

1 ($14^{1}/_{2}$-ounce) can fat-free low-sodium chicken broth

8 cups stemmed spinach leaves, in $1/2$-inch-wide strips (about 8 ounces)

$1/4$ teaspoon pepper, or to taste

$1/8$ teaspoon red pepper flakes, or to taste

Dash of salt, or to taste

$1/2$ cup freshly grated Romano cheese

GARNISH (OPTIONAL)   freshly ground black pepper

1. Bring a large pot of water to a boil over high heat; add salt, then the radiatore and the potatoes. When the water returns to a boil, stir occasionally to separate the radiatore. Reduce the heat to medium-high and cook for about 9 to 11 minutes, or according to package instructions, until the radiatore and potatoes are tender.

2. While the radiatore is cooking, heat the oil in a large nonstick skillet over medium-high heat. Add the onion and garlic; cook, stirring occasionally, for about 5 minutes or

until the onion is tender. Stir in the chicken broth and the spinach; cover and cook for about 1 minute or until the spinach is wilted. Remove from the heat and stir in the pepper, red pepper flakes, and salt.

3. When the radiatore and potatoes are done, drain well; return to the pot. Add the chicken broth-spinach mixture; toss to combine over medium heat just until heated through. Add the Romano cheese and toss again. Adjust the seasonings to taste.

PER SERVING: Cal 520/Prot 21.8g/Carb 80.1g/Fat 12.5g/Chol 0mg/Sod 639mg

Variation

•   Substitute yams (see Tip) for the yukon gold potatoes.

TIPS

Yukon gold potatoes, available in most supermarkets, have a skin and flesh that range from buttery yellow to golden. When cooked, they have a moist consistency and a rich flavor. Like other potatoes, store them in a dark, cool, well-ventilated place for up to 2 weeks. Exposure to light causes a green tinge, which can be toxic if consumed in large quantities. Warm temperatures encourage sprouting and shriveling. Refrigeration causes potatoes to become sweet and to darken when cooked.

•   Yams and sweet potatoes are plump, smooth-skinned tubers of a plant in the morning glory family; they are actually not related to potatoes at all. The distinction between yams and sweet potatoes is often confusing, and the names are often interchanged. The flesh of yams (sometimes called red sweet potatoes) is orange and quite sweet when cooked; sweet potatoes (sometimes called white sweet potatoes) have a lighter skin, and the flesh is yellow. Store both in a cool, dark, and dry place for up to 2 weeks; do not refrigerate.

chicken
and **garden vegetables**
with **penne**

Makes 6 servings

This hearty dish with a bright hint of lemon is a family favorite from my cookbook, The 15-
Minute Gourmet: Chicken. *And it's as versatile as it is quick and tasty; just follow the basic
format and use whatever pasta or vegetables you have on hand.*

8 ounces penne rigate (about 3 cups)

2 tablespoons olive oil, divided

16 ounces boneless, skinless chicken
    breast halves, cut into 1-inch squares

2 teaspoons lemon zest (see Tips)

1 tablespoon fresh lemon juice

2 tablespoons minced fresh basil, or to
    taste (or 1 teaspoon dried basil)

1/2 teaspoon pepper, or to taste

Dash of salt, or to taste

2 medium zucchini, halved lengthwise
    and cut into 1/4-inch-thick slices (about
    2 cups)

4 medium scallions, coarsely chopped

1 teaspoon minced garlic

4 plum tomatoes, halved lengthwise and
    cut into 1/4-inch-thick slices (about
    2 cups)

GARNISH (OPTIONAL)   freshly ground black pepper, freshly grated Parmesan cheese,
toasted pine nuts

1. Bring a large pot of water to a boil over high heat; add salt, then the penne. When the
    water returns to a boil, stir occasionally to separate the penne. Reduce the heat to
    medium-high and cook for about 12 to 14 minutes, or according to package instruc-
    tions, until noodles are *al dente.*

2. While the penne is cooking, heat 1 tablespoon of the oil in a large nonstick skillet over
    medium-high heat. Add the chicken; cook, stirring occasionally, for about 4 minutes or
    until it is white on the outside but not cooked through.

3. While the chicken is cooking, combine the remaining 1 tablespoon of the oil with the lemon zest, lemon juice, basil, pepper, and salt in a small bowl; set aside.

4. Add the zucchini, scallions, and garlic to the skillet; continue to cook, stirring occasionally, for about 4 more minutes or until the chicken is cooked through and the zucchini is tender. Reduce the heat to low. Add the tomatoes and the lemon juice mixture; stir gently for about 1 minutes until the tomatoes are warmed and softened. Remove from the heat.

5. When the penne is done, drain well; return to the pot. Add the chicken-vegetable mixture and toss over medium heat just until heated through. Adjust the seasonings to taste.

PER SERVING: Cal 310/Prot 27.6g/Carb 32.5g/Fat 7.7g/Chol 58mg/Sod 75mg

Variation

- Substitute other vegetables for the zucchini or tomatoes (up to 5 cups total). Try broccoli florets, cut asparagus, julienned carrots, or oil-packed sun-dried tomatoes, drained and chopped.

> ## TIPS
>
> - To zest, or to remove long, thin strips of rind from lemons, limes, or oranges, use a zester. This kitchen gadget has a short flat blade with a beveled end and five small holes. Firmly draw the blade over the fruit skin, ideally right over the dish you are preparing to catch the fragrant and flavorful oils. (If you do not have a zester, use a vegetable peeler to remove strips of the peel; cut them into thinner strips with a small knife.)
>
> - Before grating or zesting citrus rind, scrub the fruit well, then dry it thoroughly. Remove only the outer, colored part; the white portion beneath tastes bitter.

pasta shells
with **tomatoes**
and **chèvre**

Makes 4 servings

The fresh, tangy taste of chèvre cheese and its creamy texture combine beautifully with tomatoes and herbs. This dish is elegant simplicity at its best.

12 ounces medium (1/2- to 1-inch) pasta shells (about 4 1/2 cups)

1 tablespoon olive oil

1/4 cup finely chopped onion

1 teaspoon minced garlic

2 tomatoes, peeled and cut into 1-inch cubes

1/2 cup fat-free low-sodium chicken broth

1 tablespoon minced fresh thyme (or 1/2 teaspoon dried thyme)

2 teaspoons minced fresh rosemary (or 1/2 teaspoon dried rosemary, crushed)

1/2 teaspoon pepper, or to taste

Dash of salt, or to taste

3 ounces chèvre cheese (see Tip)

GARNISH (OPTIONAL)   freshly ground black pepper, sprigs of fresh thyme

1. Bring a large pot of water to a boil over high heat; add salt, then the pasta shells. When the water returns to a boil, stir occasionally to separate the shells. Reduce the heat to medium-high and cook for about 9 to 11 minutes, or according to package instructions, until noodles are *al dente*.

2. While the shells are cooking, heat the oil in a large nonstick sauté pan over medium-high heat. Add the onion and garlic; cook, stirring occasionally, for about 3 minutes or until the onion is tender. Add the tomatoes; stir for about 2 minutes or until softened. Stir in the chicken broth, thyme, rosemary, pepper, and salt; cook, stirring occasionally, for about 2 minutes. Remove from the heat and cover to keep warm.

3. When the shells are done, drain well; return to the pot. Add the chicken broth mixture and toss over medium heat until heated through. Remove from the heat. Add the chèvre cheese; stir gently until it is melted. Adjust the seasonings to taste.

PER SERVING: Cal 404/Prot 13.9g/Carb 69.2g/Fat 8g/Chol 14mg/Sod 224mg

Variation

- Before adding the chicken broth mixture, toss cooked shrimp with the pasta shells. (Shell, devein, and poach fresh shrimp or use frozen shrimp that have been thawed.)

TIP

Chèvre and Montrachet are tangy, creamy cheeses made from goat's milk. Domestic goat cheese is a fine substitute for the more expensive, imported brands. Once opened, wrap tightly in plastic wrap; store in the refrigerator for 1 to 2 weeks. (Do not confuse chèvre and Montrachet with feta cheese or *caprino,* Italian goat cheese, which is dried, less creamy, and more acidic.)

potato **gnocchi** primavera

Makes 4 servings

Potato Gnocchi (pronounced nyokee) are little dumplings made from potatoes. You'll find them in the freezer section packaged in boxes and shelved with the dried pastas in most supermarkets. Their appealing comfort-food texture serves as a base for a peppery blend of vegetables in tomato sauce.

2 tablespoons olive oil

1/2 cup coarsely chopped onion (see Tip)

1 teaspoon minced garlic

1 cup small broccoli florets

2 cups sliced mushrooms

1 (15-ounce) can diced tomatoes, with juice

1 (14-ounce) can quartered artichoke
   hearts packed in water, drained

1 cup fat-free low-sodium chicken broth

1 tablespoon minced fresh basil (or
   1 teaspoon dried basil)

1/2 teaspoon pepper, or to taste

Dash of salt, or to taste

16 ounces frozen potato gnocchi

GARNISH (OPTIONAL)   freshly ground black pepper, freshly grated Parmesan cheese

1. Bring a large pot of water to a boil over high heat.

2. Meanwhile, heat the oil in a large nonstick sauté pan over medium-high heat. Add the onion and garlic; cook, stirring constantly, for about 3 minutes or until the onion is crisp-tender. Add the broccoli; cook, stirring constantly, for about 2 minutes or until it is crisp-tender. Add the mushrooms; continue cooking, stirring constantly, for about 2 more minutes or until they are tender. Stir in the tomatoes with juice, artichoke hearts,

chicken broth, dried basil (if using), pepper, and salt. Increase the heat to high; cook, stirring occasionally, for about 5 more minutes or until the broccoli is tender and the sauce thickens slightly. Stir in the fresh basil (if using). Adjust the seasonings to taste. Cover and keep warm over very low heat.

3. When the sauce is nearly done cooking, add salt, then the gnocchi to the boiling water. When the water returns to a boil, stir occasionally to separate the gnocchi. Reduce the heat to medium-high and cook for about 2 to 4 minutes, or according to package instructions, until the gnocchi float to the top and are tender. Drain well.

4. To serve, spoon the gnocchi into 4 shallow pasta bowls; top with the vegetables and sauce.

PER SERVING: Cal 325/Prot 10.1g/Carb 54.2g/Fat 7.5g/Chol 0mg/Sod 946mg

ADVANCE PREPARATION   Covered and refrigerated, the sauce will keep for up to 2 days. Reheat and serve over hot, freshly cooked gnocchi.

Variation

• Substitute other vegetables for the broccoli and artichoke hearts (up to 3 cups total). Try cut green beans, cut asparagus, or peas.

TIPS

• Choose onions that are heavy for their size, with dry skins and no soft spots or sprouts. Stored in a cool, dry place with good air circulation, onions will keep for up to 2 months. Store them away from potatoes, because they cause each other to spoil. Onions can be refrigerated for up to a week.

• When you need only part of an onion, do not peel it before cutting. The unused portion will keep better in the refrigerator if the skin is left on. Wrap it tightly in plastic wrap or store it in a screw-top jar. If you prefer, chop leftover onion and store it in a refrigerator container or a zip-top plastic bag; use within 4 days. Frozen in a plastic bag, chopped onion will keep for several months.

• Tear-producing vapors can be reduced by refrigerating an onion for several hours or freezing it for 20 minutes before chopping.

mediterranean
pasta skillet
with **cannellini beans**

Makes 4 servings

Abundant in distinctive Mediterranean flavors, this comforting dish is hearty and nutritious; and the creamy-textured, buttery-tasting beans make the dish oh, so satisfying. Your family will clamor for seconds—guaranteed. For the best flavor and consistency, use canned diced Italian-style plum tomatoes.

8 ounces penne (about 3 cups)

1 tablespoon olive oil

1/4 cup minced shallots

2 (141/2-ounce) cans diced tomatoes, with juice

1 (19-ounce) can cannellini beans, drained and rinsed (see Tip)

1 tablespoon minced fresh oregano (or 1 teaspoon dried oregano); (see Tip)

1/2 teaspoon pepper, or to taste

Dash of salt, or to taste (optional if using feta as a garnish)

4 cups coarsely shredded stemmed spinach leaves (about 4 ounces)

GARNISH (OPTIONAL)   freshly ground black pepper, crumbled feta cheese

1. Bring a large pot of water to a boil over high heat; add salt, then the penne. When the water returns to a boil, stir occasionally to separate the penne. Reduce the heat to medium-high and cook for about 12 to 14 minutes, or according to package instructions, until noodles are *al dente*.

2. While the penne is cooking, heat the oil in a large nonstick sauté pan over medium-high heat. Add the shallots; cook, stirring constantly, for about 2 minutes or until tender but not browned. Stir in the tomatoes with juice, beans, oregano, pepper and salt. Increase the heat to high; cook, uncovered, for about 4 minutes or until the liquid

is reduced by about half. Reduce the heat to low; stir in the spinach. Cover and cook for about 2 minutes or until the spinach is wilted. Remove the pan from the heat.

3. When the penne is done, drain well. Add to the sauté pan, and stir the mixture gently over low heat just until heated through. Adjust the seasonings to taste.

PER SERVING: Cal 410/Prot 16.1g/Carb 73.8g/Fat 5.6g/Chol 0mg/Sod 659mg

ADVANCE PREPARATION   Covered and refrigerated, this dish will keep for up to 1 day. Reheat, stirring gently, over low heat or in the microwave.

TIPS

- Most supermarkets carry cannellini beans both canned and dried. They are large, white Italian kidney beans, especially popular in soups and salads.

- When stored in a tightly closed container (rather than in a box) in a dark, dry place, dried herbs will remain flavorful for about a year. (It's a good idea to date the jars when you buy them.) They should resemble the color they were when fresh, not dull or brownish-green. To get the most out of dried herbs, crumble them between your fingers to release the aromatic compounds as you add them to your recipes.

capellini with
crabmeat
and **potatoes**

Makes 6 servings

Choose this for simple, elegant entertaining. Organize the ingredients before your guests arrive, so the dish can be cooked quickly just before serving. Sometimes I top each serving with a few steamed slender asparagus spears; and, in my opinion, adding dollops of chèvre cheese is a must.

1 tablespoon olive oil	1/2 teaspoon pepper, or to taste
1/4 cup finely chopped onion	1/4 teaspoon salt, or to taste
1 teaspoon minced garlic	12 ounces capellini (angel hair pasta)
3 tomatoes, peeled and cut into 1-inch cubes (see Tip)	6 ounces frozen snow crabmeat, thawed and cut into 1-inch chunks
2 tablespoons tomato paste	1 medium scallion, finely chopped
1/2 cup dry white wine	1/4 cup coarsely chopped fresh basil
1/2 cup fat-free low-sodium chicken broth	1 tablespoon minced fresh flat-leaf parsley

GARNISH (OPTIONAL)   freshly ground black pepper, chèvre cheese, sprigs of fresh flat-leaf parsley or basil

1. Bring a large pot of water to a boil over high heat.

2. Meanwhile, heat the oil in a large nonstick sauté pan over medium-high heat. Add the onion and garlic; cook, stirring occasionally, for about 2 minutes or until the onion is tender. Stir in the tomatoes and tomato paste; cook stirring occasionally, for about 4

minutes or until the tomatoes are softened. Stir in the wine, chicken broth, pepper, and salt; cook, stirring occasionally, for about 5 more minutes or until the sauce is slightly reduced. Reduce the heat to medium.

3. Add salt, then the capellini to the pot of boiling water. When the water returns to a boil, stir occasionally to separate the capellini. Reduce the heat to medium-high and cook for about 3 to 4 minutes, or according to package instructions, until noodles are *al dente*. While the capellini is cooking, add the crabmeat, scallion, basil, and parsley to the sauté pan; stir gently until the mixture is heated through.

4. When the capellini is done, drain well; return to the pot. Add the sauce and toss gently. Adjust the seasonings to taste.

PER SERVING: Cal 272/Prot 12.4g/Carb 47.8g/Fat 3.5g/Chol 20mg/Sod 203mg

Variations

• Substitute chicken broth for the wine.

• Substitute frozen or refrigerated imitation crabmeat for the frozen snow crabmeat.

> ## TIP
>
> To peel a tomato, first core it with a paring knife, removing the stem end and white center; cut an X on the bottom of the tomato, carefully piercing just through the skin. Immerse it in a pot of boiling water just long enough to loosen the skin without cooking the tomato (5 seconds for a very ripe tomato, 10 to 20 seconds for a firmer tomato). Remove the tomato with a slotted spoon and immediately plunge it into a bowl of very cold water; let stand for about 1 minute. When the tomato is cool enough to handle, use a paring knife to slip off the skin, which will be very loose.

penne with
peppery arugula
sauce

Makes 4 servings

The peppery taste of arugula is a natural with tomatoes and feta cheese. And shallots do double duty, providing the flavors of both onion and garlic. Using just the right proportion of these few highly flavored ingredients creates a simple sauce as aromatic as it is memorable.

12 ounces penne (about 4 cups)	2 tablespoons minced fresh flat-leaf parsley
2 tablespoons olive oil	$1/2$ teaspoon sugar
$1/3$ cup minced shallots (see Tip)	$1/2$ teaspoon pepper, or to taste
1 (28-ounce) can diced tomatoes, with juice	Dash of salt, or to taste
2 cups coarsely chopped stemmed arugula leaves (see Tip)	$1/2$ cup crumbled feta cheese

GARNISH (OPTIONAL)   freshly ground black pepper

1. Bring a large pot of water to a boil over high heat; add salt, then the penne. When the water returns to a boil, stir occasionally to separate the penne. Reduce the heat to medium-high and cook for about 12 to 14 minutes, or according to package instructions, until noodles are *al dente*.

2. While the penne is cooking, heat the oil in a large nonstick sauté pan over medium-high heat. Add the shallots; cook, stirring constantly, for about 3 minutes or until tender but not browned. Stir in the tomatoes and juice; cook, stirring occasionally, for about 5 minutes or until the liquid thickens slightly. Stir in the arugula and parsley; cover and reduce the heat to low. Cook for about 2 minutes or until the arugula is wilted. Remove from the heat and stir in the sugar, pepper, and salt; cover to keep warm.

3. When the penne is done, drain well; return to the pot. Add the sauce and toss. Add the feta cheese and toss again. Adjust the seasonings to taste.

PER SERVING: Cal 514/Prot 17.7g/Carb 77.5g/Fat 14.9g/Chol 25mg/Sod 697mg

TIPS

- Shallots, a member of the onion family, are small bulbous herbs with a mild onion-garlic flavor. Always use fresh shallots; dehydrated or powdered products will not do. (If unavailable, substitute some fresh onion and fresh garlic.) Fresh shallots will keep for up to 1 month in the bottom bin of your refrigerator; use before they begin to sprout. When cooking, don't allow shallots to brown or they will taste bitter.

- Arugula, also called roquette or rocket, has long, spear-shaped leaves that resemble dandelion greens; they have a spicy, peppery, mustardlike bitterness and aroma. Select dark green leaves 3 to 5 inches long; the more mature the green, the stronger the flavor. Wrap the roots in moist paper towels and place them in a plastic bag; store in the refrigerator for up to 2 days. Wash the sandy leaves thoroughly before using.

spaghetti
puttanesca

Makes 4 servings

When researching this classic Italian dish, I learned that "puttana" means lady of the evening. This quick-to-prepare and quick-to-eat dish is the one she would use to seduce her clients. The sauce is chunky, bold, and dramatic, as you might expect.

12 ounces spaghetti

2 tablespoons olive oil

2 teaspoons minced garlic

1 (28-ounce) can Italian plum tomatoes, coarsely chopped (reserve the juice)

$1/4$ cup coarsely chopped fresh flat-leaf parsley

2 tablespoons minced fresh basil (or 1 teaspoon dried basil)

2 teaspoons minced fresh oregano (or $1/2$ teaspoon dried oregano); (see Tip)

$1/4$ teaspoon red pepper flakes, or to taste

$1/3$ cup sliced Kalamata olives (about 12 pitted olives)

1 tablespoon capers, drained and rinsed

$1/4$ teaspoon pepper, or to taste

$1/8$ teaspoon salt, or to taste

GARNISH (OPTIONAL)   freshly ground black pepper, freshly grated Parmesan cheese or crumbled feta cheese

1. Bring a large pot of water to a boil over high heat; add salt, then the spaghetti. When the water returns to a boil, stir occasionally to separate the spaghetti. Reduce the heat to medium-high and cook for about 8 to 10 minutes, or according to package instructions, until noodles are *al dente*.

2. While the spaghetti is cooking, heat the oil in a large nonstick sauté pan over medium-high heat. Add the garlic; cook, stirring constantly, for about 1 minute or until fragrant. Stir in the tomatoes with juice, parsley, basil, oregano, and red pepper flakes. Cook, stirring frequently, for about 5 minutes or until the liquid is slightly thickened. Reduce the heat to low; stir in the remaining ingredients.

3. When the spaghetti is done, drain well; return to the pot. Add the tomato sauce and toss over medium heat just until heated through. Adjust the seasonings to taste.

> **PER SERVING:** Cal 468/Prot 12.8g/Carb 76.2g/Fat 12.5g/Chol 0mg/Sod 819mg

ADVANCE PREPARATION   Covered and refrigerated, the sauce will keep for up to 2 days. Reheat and toss with hot, freshly cooked spaghetti.

Variation

•   Add 6 anchovy fillets, coarsely chopped; cook with the garlic.

> **TIP**
>
> Oregano should be used in moderation because it has a pungent flavor; this is especially true for Mexican oregano, which is stronger than Mediterranean oregano. When buying the fresh herb, look for bright green, fresh bunches with no sign of wilting or yellowing. Store it, unwashed, in a plastic bag in the refrigerator for up to 3 days.

chicken,
mushrooms, and noodles
in **honey-mustard sauce**

Makes 4 servings

For a vegetarian version, omit the chicken and substitute vegetable stock for the chicken broth; sauté an additional 2 cups sliced mushrooms and stir 2 cups steamed sliced asparagus into the completed sauce. Or for the perfect dish to welcome spring, use 3 cups fresh morels (see Tips); sauté with the shallots in 1 tablespoon olive oil for about 3 minutes and stir in the Honey-Mustard Sauce.

1 tablespoon olive oil

12 ounces boneless skinless chicken
    breast halves, cut into 2-inch-long by
    $1/2$-inch-wide strips

Honey-Mustard Sauce

$1/4$ cup Dijon mustard (see Tip)

3 tablespoons honey

$1/2$ cup half-and-half

$1/2$ cup fat-free low-sodium chicken broth

1 tablespoon minced fresh tarragon (or
    $1/2$ teaspoon dried tarragon)

$1/4$ teaspoon pepper, or to taste

Dash of salt or to taste

To Complete the Recipe

8 ounces medium egg noodles (about
    4 cups)

2 cups sliced mushrooms, preferably cremini

$1/4$ cup minced shallots

GARNISH (OPTIONAL)   freshly ground black pepper, minced fresh flat-leaf parsley

1. Bring a large pot of water to a boil over high heat.

2. Meanwhile, heat the oil in a large nonstick sauté pan over medium-high heat. Add the chicken; cook, stirring occasionally, for about 4 minutes or until it is white on the outside but not cooked through.

3. While the chicken is cooking, prepare the sauce: Combine the mustard and honey in a small bowl. Stir in the remaining ingredients; set aside.

4. When the water comes to a boil, add salt, then the noodles. When the water returns to a boil, stir occasionally to separate the noodles. Reduce the heat to medium-high and cook for about 5 to 7 minutes, or according to package instructions, until noodles are *al dente*.

5. Add the mushrooms and shallots to the sauté pan; continue to cook, stirring constantly, for about 5 more minutes or until the chicken is lightly browned and cooked through and the mushrooms are tender. Reduce the heat to low; add the sauce and stir just until warm. (Do not allow the sauce to come to a boil.) Remove from the heat and cover to keep warm.

6. When the noodles are done, drain well; return to the pot. Add the chicken-sauce mixture; toss over medium heat just until heated through. Adjust the seasonings to taste.

PER SERVING: Cal 479/Prot 35.1g/Carb 57.2g/Fat 12.2g/Chol 132mg/Sod 237mg

---

TIPS

- Morels are edible wild mushrooms belonging to the same fungus species as the truffle. Choose fresh mushrooms with a firm yet spongy texture. Refrigerate them in a single layer covered with a damp towel

- Dried morels, available year-round, have a more intense, smokier flavor than fresh morels. They can be substituted in recipes after being rehydrated (soak in warm water for 30 minutes or boil for 2 to 5 minutes; for maximum flavor, use only as much water as the mushrooms will absorb). To remove traces of sand, both fresh and dried morels should be rinsed before use.

- Dijon mustard, which originated in Dijon, France, is made from brown mustard seeds, spices, and white wine, making it more flavorful (and more expensive) than ordinary yellow mustard.

shrimp and penne
in spicy tomato sauce

Makes 4 servings

This spicy herb-and-garlic-flavored dish is one of my favorite standbys for entertaining. I like to shell and devein the shrimp, leaving the tails on. The presentation is eye-catching; the only downside is that the shrimp are a bit messy to eat!

12 ounces penne (about 4 cups)

Spicy Tomato Sauce

1 (14^1/$_2$-ounce) can Italian-style stewed tomatoes (see Tip)

2 tablespoons fresh lemon juice

1 tablespoon olive oil

1 teaspoon minced garlic

1 teaspoon Hungarian paprika (see Tip)

^{1}/$_2$ teaspoon pepper, or to taste

^{1}/$_4$ teaspoon salt, or to taste

^{1}/$_8$ teaspoon cayenne, or to taste

1 teaspoon minced fresh oregano (or ^{1}/$_2$ teaspoon dried oregano)

1 teaspoon minced fresh rosemary (or ^{1}/$_2$ teaspoon dried rosemary, crushed)

To Complete the Recipe

1 tablespoon butter

8 ounces medium shrimp (about 20), shelled and deveined

2 bay leaves

GARNISH (OPTIONAL)   freshly grated Parmesan cheese or crumbled feta cheese

1. Bring a large pot of water to a boil over high heat; add salt, then the penne. When the water returns to a boil, stir occasionally to separate the penne.

Reduce the heat to medium-high and cook for about 12 to 14 minutes, or according to package instructions, until noodles are *al dente*.

2. While the penne is cooking, put the sauce ingredients (except the oregano and rosemary) into a food processor; process until the mixture is smooth. Stir in the oregano and rosemary.

3. When the pasta is nearly done, melt the butter in a large nonstick sauté pan over medium-high heat. Stir in the sauce and bay leaves; heat until the sauce is bubbly. Add the shrimp; cook, stirring and constantly turning the shrimp, for about 2 to 3 minutes or until they are cooked through. Remove the pan from the heat; remove and discard the bay leaves. Use a slotted spoon to transfer the shrimp to a bowl; cover to keep warm.

4. When the penne is done, drain well; return to the pot. Add the sauce and toss. Adjust the seasonings to taste.

5. Serve the penne in shallow pasta bowls; arrange the shrimp on top of each serving.

PER SERVING: Cal 466/Prot 23.2g/Carb 72.7g/Fat 9.2g/Chol 95mg/Sod 467mg

ADVANCE PREPARATION   The sauce can be made up to 2 days in advance; cover and refrigerate. Reheat the sauce, cook the shrimp, and cook the penne just before serving.

Variation

- Omit the shrimp and the bay leaves. Melt the butter in a large nonstick saucepan over medium-high heat; add the Spicy Tomato Sauce and heat until bubbly. Stir in 4 cups coarsely shredded stemmed spinach leaves. Reduce the heat to medium, cover, and simmer for about 2 minutes or until the spinach is wilted; toss with the cooked penne.

TIPS

- When buying canned tomatoes, read the labels. Some tomatoes are canned whole. Others are diced (recipe-ready tomatoes); select these for recipes calling for chopped canned tomatoes. Other canned tomatoes contain herbs and seasonings, such as stewed tomatoes. "Italian tomatoes" is the labeling for whole plum tomatoes. In cooked dishes, canned tomatoes are usually preferable to fresh tomatoes of poor quality.

- Paprika is a powder made by grinding aromatic sweet red pepper pods. Most paprika comes from Spain, South America, California, or Hungary; the Hungarian variety is considered by many to be the best. Hungarian paprika comes in three levels of hotness: mild (also called "sweet"), hot, and exceptionally hot. To preserve the color and flavor, store paprika in a cool, dark place for no longer than 6 months.

spaghettini
with **baby** peas

Makes 4 servings

This simple recipe relies on a short list of ingredients, so superior quality—especially top-notch Parmesan cheese—is of the utmost importance. If you'd like, toss in strips of chicken breast or butterflied shrimp that have been sautéed in olive oil; or, if time permits, grill chicken breasts, cut them into diagonal strips, and arrange them atop the spaghettini mixture. For a quick weeknight dinner, simply drain a 6-ounce can of water-packed solid white albacore tuna, flake, and toss with the spaghettini.

12 ounces spaghettini

1 tablespoon olive oil

1 tablespoon minced garlic

$1/2$ cup fat-free low-sodium chicken broth

1 cup frozen baby peas, thawed (see Tip)

$1/2$ teaspoon pepper, or to taste

$1/8$ teaspoon salt, or to taste

$1/2$ cup freshly grated Parmesan cheese
  (see Tips)

2 tablespoons butter

GARNISH (OPTIONAL)   freshly ground black pepper, freshly grated Parmesan cheese

1. Bring a large pot of water to a boil over high heat; add salt, then the spaghettini. When the water returns to a boil, stir occasionally to separate the spaghettini. Reduce the heat to medium-high and cook for about 8 to 10 minutes, or according to package instructions, until noodles are *al dente*.

2. While the spaghettini is cooking, heat the oil in a large nonstick sauté pan over medium-high heat. Add the garlic; cook, stirring constantly, for about 30 seconds

or until fragrant. Add the chicken broth, peas, pepper, and salt; stir gently for about 1 minute or until heated through. Remove from the heat.

3. When the spaghettini is done, drain well; return to the pot. Add the chicken broth mixture; toss gently over medium heat until heated through. Add the Parmesan and butter; toss just until the butter is melted. Adjust the seasonings to taste.

PER SERVING: Cal 492/Prot 18.7g/Carb 71.8g/Fat 14.4g/Chol 25mg/Sod 437mg

Variation

- Substitute steamed broccoli florets or cut asparagus for the peas.

TIPS

- Generally, the flavor of frozen baby peas (or petit pois) is preferable to that of the standard-size peas. Harvested when young, baby peas remain especially sweet after picking; they also retain a brighter green color and a firmer texture.

- Always buy freshly grated Parmesan or, better yet, grate your own from a block of Parmesan using a hand grater or a food processor; if you prefer, slice it into thin slivers at the table or just before serving.

- The best quality Parmesan cheese is Italy's Parmigiano-Reggiano. It is available in specialty cheese stores, Italian markets, and many supermarkets.

- Sealed in a tightly closed container, freshly grated Parmesan will keep in the refrigerator for up to a week. It can be frozen; however, the flavor and texture will deteriorate. Wrapped tightly in plastic wrap and refrigerated, a block of Parmesan will keep for up to 4 weeks. Changing the cheese's wrapper occasionally will extend its life even longer.

vermicelli
with **clam** sauce

Makes 4 servings

This is a light, brothy clam sauce fragrant with garlic and olive oil; it is bold in flavor and elegant in its simplicity. With canned clams from your pantry and a few other staples, you can make this on a moment's notice.

12 ounces vermicelli

Clam Sauce

2 tablespoons olive oil, divided

2 tablespoons diced onion

2 teaspoons minced garlic

2 (6-ounce) cans minced or chopped clams, with juice

1/2 cup dry white wine

1/4 teaspoon red pepper flakes, or to taste

1/4 teaspoon pepper, or to taste

Dash of salt, or to taste

1/2 cup dry bread crumbs (see Tip)

1/4 cup minced fresh flat-leaf parsley

GARNISH (OPTIONAL)   freshly ground black pepper, freshly grated Parmesan cheese

1. Bring a large pot of water to a boil over high heat; add salt, then the vermicelli. When the water returns to a boil, stir occasionally to separate the vermicelli. Reduce the heat to medium-high and cook for about 9 to 11 minutes, or according to package instructions, until noodles are *al dente*.

2. While the vermicelli is cooking, heat 1 tablespoon of the oil in a large nonstick sauté pan over medium-high heat. Add the onion and garlic; cook, stirring constantly, for about 2 minutes or until tender but not browned. Stir in the clams with their juice,

wine, red pepper flakes, pepper, and salt. Cook, stirring occasionally, for about 2 minutes or until bubbly. Reduce the heat to medium; simmer, uncovered, for about 5 minutes.

3. Meanwhile, heat the remaining 1 tablespoon of oil in a small nonstick skillet over medium heat. Add the bread crumbs and stir for about 2 to 3 minutes or until lightly browned. Remove from the heat; stir in the parsley.

4. When the vermicelli is done, drain well; return to the pot. Add the clam sauce and toss over medium heat just until heated through. Adjust the seasonings to taste.

5. To serve, divide the mixture among pasta bowls; sprinkle with the bread crumbs.

   PER SERVING: Cal 469/Prot 18.9g/Carb 78.3g/Fat 8.9g/Chol 15mg/Sod 626mg

> ### TIP
>
> Making dry bread crumbs is an ideal use for day-old bread, especially French baguettes. When using a loaf of whole wheat or white bread, begin by removing the crusts. If the bread is not dry, place a single layer of bread slices on a baking sheet and toast in a 200°F oven for about 10 to 15 minutes or until the slices are thoroughly dried and lightly browned. After cooling, process them in your food processor until the bread crumbs are the desired consistency. Packaged dry bread crumbs can also be purchased at the supermarket. Check the labeling; some bread crumbs are seasoned.

roasted
asparagus-
pasta **toss**

Makes 4 servings

Here's the perfect choice for a light dinner to celebrate the arrival of spring. Even though asparagus is available in most supermarkets year-round, the thin and tender, early spring bunches are best for this recipe. Serve this as an accompaniment to chicken breasts grilled outdoors or diagonally slice the chicken into strips and arrange them atop the servings of pasta. (For summer ease, roast the asparagus on the outdoor grill, too.)

12 ounces penne rigate (about 4 cups)

1 tablespoon olive oil

Dash of pepper, or to taste

Dash of salt, or to taste

1 pound thin asparagus spears, diagonally
   cut into 2-inch-long pieces

1 cup fat-free low-sodium chicken broth

1 tablespoon butter

2 teaspoons lemon zest

2 tablespoons fresh lemon juice

$1/4$ cup toasted pine nuts

2 tablespoon snipped fresh chives (see Tip)

GARNISH (OPTIONAL)   freshly ground black pepper, crumbled feta cheese

1. Preheat the oven to 400°F.

2. Bring a large pot of water to a boil over high heat; add salt, then the penne. When the water returns to a boil, stir occasionally to separate the penne. Reduce the heat to medium-high and cook for about 12 to 14 minutes, or according to package instructions, until noodles are *al dente*.

3. While the penne is cooking, combine the oil, pepper, and salt in a medium bowl. Add the asparagus and toss. Place the asparagus in a single layer on a baking sheet. Roast in the preheated oven, tossing or stirring the asparagus several times, for about 15 minutes or until it is tender and lightly browned. (If the asparagus is very thin, reduce the cooking time by several minutes and check often to prevent burning.)

4. While the penne and asparagus are cooking, combine the chicken broth, butter, lemon zest, and lemon juice in a small saucepan over medium heat. Heat, stirring occasionally, until the butter is melted.

5. When the penne is done, drain well; return to the pot. Add the asparagus and the pine nuts; toss. Gently toss in the chicken broth mixture over medium heat just until heated through. Adjust the seasonings to taste. Toss in the chives just before serving.

PER SERVING: Cal 476/Prot 15.5g/Carb 71.9g/Fat/ 14.1g/Chol 8mg/Sod 229mg

---

TIPS

- Chives are a delicately flavored member of the onion family. Given a choice, buy potted chives; they are fresher than cut. Use scissors to snip off what you need, cutting off whole blades rather than chopping the tops off all the blades. If you buy cut chives, look for those with a uniform green color and no signs of wilting; wrap them in damp paper towels, seal in a plastic bag, and refrigerate for up to 1 week. When using in cooked dishes, add chives near the end of the cooking time to retain their flavor. Avoid dried chopped chives, which have lost their characteristic flavor and aroma. If fresh chives are unavailable, substitute scallion greens cut into julienne strips.

- Julienne refers to cutting foods into thin, about $1/8$-inch-wide, matchstick strips.

long fusilli
with **ratatouille**

Makes 4 servings

Eggplant's called "the king of vegetables" for a good reason. It allows you to create a hearty sauce without meat. The chunky sauce is compatible with a toothsome and visually interesting pasta, such as long fusilli (spiral twists) or perciatelli (hollow spaghettilike pasta). I especially like to garnish the servings with dollops of creamy goat cheese; everyone loves the flavor, texture, and aroma as it melts into the eggplant sauce.

12 ounces long fusilli

2 tablespoons olive oil

1 pound unpeeled eggplant, cut into 2-inch-long, 1/4-inch-thick, by 1/2-inch-wide strips (about 4 cups); (see Tip)

1/2 cup coarsely chopped onion

1/2 cup coarsely chopped green bell pepper

2 teaspoons minced garlic

3 medium tomatoes, cut into 1/2-inch cubes (about 3 cups)

1 tablespoon capers, drained and rinsed

1 tablespoon finely chopped fresh oregano (or 1/2 teaspoon dried oregano)

1/2 teaspoon pepper, or to taste

1/4 teaspoon salt, or to taste

GARNISH (OPTIONAL)   freshly ground black pepper, toasted pine nuts, freshly grated Parmesan cheese, feta cheese, or chèvre cheese

1. Bring a large pot of water to a boil over high heat; add salt, then the fusilli. When the water returns to a boil, stir occasionally to separate the fusilli. Reduce the heat to medium-high and cook for about 8 to 10 minutes, or according to package instructions, until noodles are *al dente*.

2. Meanwhile, heat the oil in a large nonstick sauté pan over medium-high heat. Add the eggplant, onion, bell pepper, and garlic; cook, stirring occasionally, for about 5 to 6 minutes or until the eggplant is nearly tender and lightly browned. Reduce the heat to medium; stir in the tomatoes, capers, oregano, pepper, and salt. Cook, stirring occasionally, for about 3 minutes or until the tomatoes are softened. Adjust the seasonings to taste.

3. When the pasta is done, drain well. Transfer to shallow pasta bowls; top the servings with the eggplant sauce.

PER SERVING: Cal 448/Prot 12.9g/Carb 79.1g/Fat 8.9g/Chol 0mg/Sod 173mg

Variation

• Substitute Italian or baby eggplant; cut into $1/4$-inch-thick slices.

> **TIP**
>
> Eggplant does not necessarily need to be sliced, salted, and weighted to squeeze out the juice, as some cookbooks recommend. Only overripe fruit is tough and bitter, so select young, smaller eggplants. Store them in a plastic bag in the refrigerator for up to 2 weeks. The peel is edible, so it is not necessary to remove it, unless you choose to peel it for the sake of appearance or texture. Eggplant is very porous and soaks up oil like a sponge; keep fat to a minimum by using a nonstick pan, making sure the pan is very hot before adding the eggplant, and tossing and turning the eggplant as it cooks to coat all pieces evenly with the oil.

rigatoni
with swiss chard
and **bell peppers**

Makes 4 servings

Swiss chard is a leafy green vegetable you may have noticed in the produce department but have never used. I usually select rhubarb chard, a more colorful variety with bright red stems and veins. Here's a delicious way to give it a try and to reap its nutritional benefits. Leafy greens, such as Swiss chard and kale, are excellent sources of vitamins A (in the form of beta carotene) and C, as well as iron, magnesium, and potassium.

12 ounces rigatoni (about 5 cups)

2 tablespoons olive oil

1 red bell pepper, cut into 1-inch-long by
   1/2-inch-wide strips

1/4 cup coarsely chopped onion

1 teaspoon minced garlic

1 cup fat-free low-sodium chicken broth

8 cups coarsely chopped Swiss chard
   leaves (about 8 ounces); (see Tip)

1 tablespoon butter

1/2 teaspoon pepper, or to taste

2 tablespoons balsamic vinegar

1/4 teaspoon salt, or to taste

1/4 cup freshly grated Parmesan cheese

GARNISH (OPTIONAL) freshly ground black pepper

1. Bring a large pot of water to a boil over high heat; add salt, then the rigatoni. When the water returns to a boil, stir occasionally to separate the rigatoni. Reduce the heat to medium-high and cook for about 12 to 14 minutes, or according to package instructions, until noodles are *al dente*.

2. While the rigatoni is cooking, heat the oil in a large nonstick sauté pan over medium-high heat. Add the bell pepper, onion, and garlic; cook, stirring occasionally, for about 5 minutes or until the bell pepper is crisp-tender. Reduce the heat to medium; stir in

the chicken broth, chard, butter, and pepper; cover and cook for about 5 minutes or until the chard and the bell pepper are tender. Remove the pan from the heat; stir in the balsamic vinegar and salt.

3. When the rigatoni is done, drain well; return to the pot. Add the chard mixture and toss. Add the Parmesan cheese and toss again. Adjust the seasonings to taste.

PER SERVING: Cal 465/Prot 15.6g/Carb 71.1g/Fat 13.1g/Chol 13mg/Sod 537mg

TIP

Swiss chard is a member of the beet family. Choose crisp bunches with dark green, tender leaves and crisp stems. Store them refrigerated, in a plastic bag for up to 3 days. Both the large, crinkly leaves and celerylike stalks can be eaten; the dark leaves have a full-bodied texture and a distinctive flavor, similar to spinach. Rhubarb chard, with dark green leaves on reddish stalks, has a stronger flavor. Avoid using salt in the water in which you simmer or steam Swiss chard, or it will darken.

ruby
red **penne**

Makes 4 servings

Beets are a vegetable that suffers from a questionable reputation and therefore are often over-looked. I encourage you to try beets for their unique flavor and brilliant color, and I guarantee you'll be pleasantly surprised. Fresh beets require 45 minutes to bake or about 25 minutes to boil; and you must remove the skins after cooking. Canned beets are an acceptable alternative for efficient 15-minute cooking.

12 ounces penne (about 4 cups)

1 tablespoon olive oil

$^1/_2$ cup finely chopped onion

2 teaspoons minced garlic

1 (15-ounce) can diced beets with juice

$^1/_4$ cup currants (see Tip)

2 tablespoons fresh lemon juice

$^1/_2$ teaspoon pepper, or to taste

$^1/_4$ teaspoon salt, or to taste

2 teaspoons snipped fresh dill (or
   $^1/_2$ teaspoon dried dill); (see Tip)

GARNISH (OPTIONAL)   freshly ground black pepper, crumbled feta cheese, toasted coarsely chopped walnuts

1.   Bring a large pot of water to a boil over high heat; add salt, then the penne. When the water returns to a boil, stir occasionally to separate the penne. Reduce the heat to medium-high and cook for about 12 to 14 minutes, or according to package instructions, until noodles are *al dente*.

2.   While the penne is cooking, heat the oil in a large nonstick sauté pan over medium-high heat. Add the onion and garlic; cook, stirring occasionally, for about 3 minutes or until the onion is tender. Stir in the beets and juice, currants, lemon juice, pepper, salt, and

dried dill (if using). Cook, stirring occasionally, for about 3 to 5 minutes or until the currants are softened and the liquid is reduced by about half. Stir in the fresh dill (if using). Remove from the heat and cover.

3. When the penne is done, drain well; return to the pot. Add the beet mixture and toss gently over medium heat until the mixture is heated through and the pasta is evenly colored. Adjust the seasonings to taste.

PER SERVING: Cal 418/Prot 11.5g/Carb 81.8g/Fat 5g/Chol 0mg/Sod 410mg

TIPS

- About $1/4$ the size of raisins, currants are less sweet but have a stronger flavor. In the supermarket they are found among the raisins and other dried fruits.

- Dill is a sharply aromatic herb with a mild, lemony taste. When using fresh dill, cut the feathery dill tips with scissors. Dried dill is acceptable, but it is stronger than fresh, so use it in moderation.

spaghetti with mushrooms and **eggs**

Makes 4 servings

Mushroom lovers, this one's for you! Serve this simple and comforting entrée to pick up your spirits on a weeknight. For color, add a green vegetable such as steamed green beans or broccoli florets.

12 ounces spaghetti	1 cup coarsely chopped red bell pepper
3 eggs, lightly beaten (see Tips)	1/2 cup coarsely chopped onion
2 tablespoons water	1 teaspoon minced garlic
1/2 teaspoon pepper, or to taste	1/4 cup freshly grated Parmesan cheese
Dash of salt, or to taste	2 tablespoons finely chopped fresh
2 tablespoons olive oil, divided	flat-leaf parsley
3 cups sliced mushrooms	

GARNISH (OPTIONAL)   freshly ground black pepper, sprigs of fresh flat-leaf parsley

1. Bring a large pot of water to a boil over high heat; add salt, then the spaghetti. When the water returns to a boil, stir occasionally to separate the spaghetti. Reduce the heat to medium-high and cook for about 8 to 10 minutes, or according to package instructions, until noodles are *al dente*.

2. While the noodles are cooking, whisk together the eggs, water, pepper, and salt; set aside. Heat 1 tablespoon of the oil in a large nonstick skillet over medium-high heat. Add the mushrooms, bell pepper, onion, and garlic. Cook, stirring occasionally, for about 5 minutes or until tender. Add the egg mixture; cook, stirring constantly, for about 2 minutes or until the eggs are set. Remove from the heat; cover to keep warm.

3. When the spaghetti is done, drain well. Return to the pot and toss with the remaining 1 tablespoon of oil. Add the egg mixture, Parmesan cheese, and parsley; toss. Adjust the seasonings to taste.

PER SERVING: Cal 304/Prot 13.5g/Carb 32.4g/Fat 13.4g/Chol 165mg/Sod 202mg

Variation

- Substitute $3/4$ cup cholesterol-free egg substitute for the eggs; omit the water.

TIPS

With proper care and handling, eggs pose no greater health risk than other perishable foods. Since salmonella bacteria is found in some eggs, it is wise to take the following precautions:

- Buy only clean, uncracked eggs that have been refrigerated.

- Do not leave eggs in any form at room temperature for more than 2 hours.

- Cook eggs until no visible liquid remains.

- Although eggs will keep for up to 1 month in the refrigerator, they lose their fresh flavor after 1 week. Store them with the large end up in the coldest part of your refrigerator, not in the molded door rack. Since eggs can absorb odors through their porous shells, storing eggs in the carton helps protect them from the aromas of other foods.

- Cholesterol-free egg substitutes are made from real egg whites. The flavor is enhanced by the addition of a small amount of corn oil, and some yellow coloring is added to give the appearance of whole eggs. Reduced-cholesterol egg products are made from whole eggs from which nearly all of the cholesterol has been removed.

penne with hearty tomato-sage sauce

Makes 4 servings

"Rigate" desribes the ridged shape of some pastas that helps the sauce adhere to the surface of the noodles. Since shapes such as rotini and rotelle serve the same purpose, you may use these to vary the presentation of this tasty dish.

12 ounces penne rigate (about 4 cups)

Tomato-Sage Sauce

1 tablespoon olive oil

1/2 cup finely chopped celery

1/2 cup finely chopped green bell pepper

1/4 cup finely chopped shallots

1 (28-ounce) can crushed tomatoes in tomato purée

2 cups sliced mushrooms

1 teaspoon crushed dried sage leaves (or 1/2 teaspoon rubbed sage); (see Tips)

1/2 teaspoon sugar

1/2 teaspoon pepper, or to taste

1/4 teaspoon salt, or to taste

2 tablespoons minced fresh flat-leaf parsley

GARNISH (OPTIONAL)   freshly ground black pepper, freshly grated Parmesan cheese, sprigs of fresh flat-leaf parsley

1. Bring a large pot of water to a boil over high heat; add salt, then the penne. When the water returns to a boil, stir occasionally to separate the penne. Reduce the heat to medium-high and cook for about 12 to 14 minutes, or according to package instructions, until noodles are *al dente*.

2. While the penne is cooking, heat the oil in a large nonstick sauté pan over medium-high heat. Add the celery, bell pepper, and shallots; cook, stirring occasionally, for about 3 minutes or until crisp-tender. Stir in the remaining sauce ingredients, except the parsley. Increase the heat to high; cook, stirring occasionally, for about 5 minutes or until the sauce thickens slightly and the vegetables are tender. Stir in the parsley.

3. When the penne is done, drain well; return to the pot. Add the sauce and toss over medium heat just until heated through. Adjust the seasonings to taste.

PER SERVING: Cal 218/Prot 5.6g/Carb 38.7g/Fat 4.5g/Chol 28mg/Sod 644mg

ADVANCE PREPARATION   Covered and refrigerated, the sauce will keep for up to 2 days. Warm the sauce and toss with hot, freshly cooked penne.

TIPS

- Dried sage comes whole, crumbled, and ground to a powder (rubbed). Store it in a cool place for up to 6 months.

- Thyme, savory, bay leaf, rosemary, sage, oregano, and marjoram are considered to be the "robust herbs," with tough leaves that are resistant to cold weather and to heat—of the sun, and of cooking. They are strong in aroma and hearty in flavor.

- Definitions of several common terms:

   chop—to cut food into uniform shapes of small size, usually $1/2$ inch to 1 inch

   dice—to cut food into small cubes or squares $1/8$ inch to $1/4$ inch

   mince—to cut pieces of food into very small bits, no larger than $1/8$-inch square; often used for fresh herbs

farfalle crowned with
brie and pears

Makes 4 servings

When the Brie cheese melts into the warm pasta, its distinctive flavor marries with fresh pears to create a memorable (but not low-fat) dish for special occasions.

12 ounces farfalle (bow tie pasta); (about 5 cups)

1 (6-ounce) jar olive oil-packed julienned sun-dried tomatoes (1 cup); drain and reserve oil

3 tablespoons olive oil (or use reserved oil from the sun-dried tomatoes)

2 pears (at room temperature), peeled and cut into $1/2$-inch cubes (about $2^1/2$ cups); (see Tip)

4 ounces Brie cheese, coarsely chopped (about $2/3$ cup); remove and discard rind, then chop cheese (see Tips)

$1/4$ cup fresh basil chiffonade

1 tablespoon balsamic vinegar

2 teaspoons minced garlic

$1/4$ teaspoon pepper, or to taste

Dash of salt, or to taste

GARNISH (OPTIONAL)   freshly ground black pepper, toasted coarsely chopped walnuts

1. Bring a large pot of water to a boil over high heat; add salt, then the farfalle. When the water returns to a boil, stir occasionally to separate the farfalle. Reduce the heat to medium-high and cook for about 12 to 14 minutes, or according to package instructions, until noodles are *al dente*.

2. While the farfalle is cooking, stir together the remaining ingredients in a medium bowl.

3. When the farfalle is done, drain well; return to the pot. Add the pear mixture and toss. Adjust the seasonings to taste.

PER SERVING: Cal 603/Prot 22.1g/Carb 92.2g/Fat 16.2g/Chol 15mg/Sod 224mg

TIPS

- Ripen pears on your kitchen counter in a paper bag; this may require 2 to 7 days. Once ripe, they will keep for 3 to 5 days in the refrigerator. Somewhat underripe pears are best for cooking and baking.

- Brie, a soft ripened cheese made from raw or pasteurized, whole or skim milk, has an edible white rind (that may have pale brown edges) and a cream-colored interior. For the best flavor, choose Brie from France, and because its shelf life is short, use it within a few days.

- Fresh and soft-ripened cheeses should be tightly wrapped; they will keep in the coldest part of the refrigerator for up to 2 weeks. Discard fresh or soft-ripened cheeses that become moldy. Firm, semifirm, and semisoft cheeses should be wrapped airtight in a plastic bag; store in the refrigerator cheese compartment (or warmest location) for up to several weeks. Mold may be cut away if it develops. All cheeses taste best if brought to room temperature before serving.

penne with
winter fruit
in **red wine**

Makes 4 servings

Use minced fresh rosemary to achieve the most satisfying flavor; but if you only have the dried herb on hand, you can enhance the flavor and improve the texture by crushing the leaves between your fingers before adding them to the recipe. Rosemary has a bold taste, especially in dried form, so use it sparingly. Immediately after preparing, serve this peppery, fruity side dish as an accompaniment to grilled or broiled fish or chicken.

12 ounces penne (about 4 cups)

Red Wine Sauce

2 tablespoons olive oil

1 tablespoon minced garlic

1 cup dry red wine, such as Cabernet Sauvignon

3/4 cup packaged coarsely chopped dried fruit mix (including such fruits as apricots, peaches, dates, apples, papaya); (see Tip)

2 teaspoons minced fresh rosemary (or 1/2 teaspoon dried rosemary, crushed)

1/2 teaspoon pepper, or to taste

GARNISH (OPTIONAL)   minced fresh flat-leaf parsley

1. Bring a large pot of water to a boil over high heat; add salt, then the penne. When the water returns to a boil, stir occasionally to separate the penne. Reduce the heat to medium-high and cook for about 12 to 14 minutes, or according to package instructions, until noodles are *al dente*.

2. While the penne is cooking, heat the oil in a medium nonstick saucepan over medium-high heat. Add the garlic; cook, stirring constantly, for about 30 seconds or until fragrant. Stir in the remaining sauce ingredients; cook uncovered, stirring occasionally, for about 10 minutes or until the fruit is softened and the wine is reduced by about half (see Tip). Remove from the heat and cover to keep warm.

3. When the penne is done, drain well; return to the pot. Add the sauce and toss over medium heat just until heated through. Adjust the seasoning to taste.

PER SERVING: Cal 460/Prot 11.8g/Carb 84.5g/Fat 8.3g/Chol 0mg/Sod 4mg

TIPS

- Most dried fruit can be stored at room temperature for up to 1 year tightly wrapped in a plastic bag.

- Stocks and sauces are "reduced" by boiling rapidly, uncovered, until the volume is lessened by evaporation. This thickens the consistency and intensifies the flavors.

spaghetti with
tomato-basil sauce

Makes 4 servings

This simple and healthful (it's fat-free) weeknight entrée is a real kid pleaser. To suit the adults, add extra red pepper flakes to the sauce and garnish the servings with top-quality freshly grated Parmesan or Romano cheese.

12 ounces spaghetti

Tomato-Basil Sauce

1 (29-ounce) can chunky tomato sauce (or crushed tomatoes in thick tomato purée); (see Tips)

1/4 cup minced fresh basil

1/2 teaspoon sugar

1/2 teaspoon pepper, or to taste

1/8 teaspoon red pepper flakes, or to taste

Dash of salt, or to taste

GARNISH (OPTIONAL)   freshly ground black pepper, freshly grated Parmesan cheese

1. Bring a large pot of water to a boil over high heat; add salt, then the spaghetti. When the water returns to a boil, stir occasionally to separate the spaghetti. Reduce the heat to medium-high and cook for about 8 to 10 minutes, or according to package instructions, until noodles are *al dente.*

2. While the spaghetti is cooking, combine the sauce ingredients in a medium nonstick saucepan over medium heat. Heat, stirring occasionally, until hot and bubbly. Remove from the heat; cover and set aside. Adjust the seasonings to taste.

3. When the spaghetti is done, drain well. Transfer it to pasta bowls; top each serving with the sauce.

PER SERVING: Cal 367/Prot 10.8g/Carb 77.4g/Fat 1.6g/Chol 0mg/Sod 542mg

ADVANCE PREPARATION   This sauce improves in flavor if it is made 1 or 2 days in advance; cover and refrigerate. (The hotness of red pepper flakes increases as the mixture sets.) Reheat, stirring gently over medium heat, before serving atop hot, freshly cooked spaghetti.

TIPS

- Canned tomato purée is made from tomatoes that have been cooked and strained, resulting in a thick liquid. Canned tomato sauce has a slightly thinner consistency.

- Avoid cooking tomatoes in untreated aluminum or cast-iron pans. A chemical reaction will give the tomatoes a brownish color and will affect the flavor.

penne with
mexican chili sauce

Makes 4 servings

Although the list of ingredients may seem long, this sauce is exceptionally simple to prepare. This makes a great choice for a chilly night when your family is announcing, "We're hungry. What's for dinner?"

12 ounces penne (about 4 cups)

Mexican Chili Sauce

1 tablespoon olive oil

1/2 cup diced green bell pepper

1/2 cup finely chopped onion

1 teaspoon minced garlic

1 (15-ounce) can diced tomatoes, with juice

1 (15-ounce) can black beans, drained and rinsed (see Tip)

1 cup frozen corn, thawed

1 (4-ounce) can diced green chilies, drained

2 teaspoons chili powder, or to taste (see Tip)

2 teaspoons minced fresh oregano (or 1/2 teaspoon dried oregano)

1/2 teaspoon ground cumin (see Tip)

1/4 teaspoon pepper, or to taste

1/4 cup coarsely chopped fresh cilantro (do not use dried cilantro; if fresh is unavailable, substitute fresh flat-leaf parsley)

GARNISH (OPTIONAL)   freshly ground black pepper, shredded Cheddar cheese, sprigs of fresh cilantro

1. Bring a large pot of water to a boil over high heat; add salt, then the penne. When the water returns to a boil, stir occasionally to separate the penne. Reduce the heat to

medium-high and cook for about 12 to 14 minutes, or according to package instructions, until noodles are *al dente*.

2. While the penne is cooking, heat the oil in a large nonstick sauté pan over medium-high heat. Add the bell pepper, onion, and garlic; cook, stirring occasionally, for about 6 minutes or until tender but not browned. Add the remaining ingredients, except the fresh cilantro. Stir gently for about 4 minutes or until heated through.

3. When the penne is done, drain well; return the penne to the pot. Add the sauce and the cilantro; toss over medium heat just until heated through. Adjust the seasonings to taste.

PER SERVING: Cal 580/Prot 23.1g/Carb 105.8g/Fat 6.2g/Chol 0mg/Sod 605mg

ADVANCE PREPARATION   Covered and refrigerated, the sauce will keep for up to 2 days; it reheats well. Warm the sauce and toss with hot, freshly cooked penne.

Variation

•   Substitute kidney beans for the black beans.

TIPS

•   Black beans, also called turtle beans, are a member of the kidney bean family. Black on the outside, cream-colored within, they keep their shape and sweet, hearty flavor after cooking. Canned black beans are available in most supermarkets.

•   In Mexican markets, chili powder is simply a powdered form of ancho, pasilla, or other dried red chile peppers. The domestic varieties often contain extra seasonings such as cumin, oregano, garlic, ground coriander, black pepper, and paprika. If you want to make your chili powder hotter, just add cayenne.

•   Cumin is the dried fruit of a plant in the parsley family. Available in both seed and ground forms, it provides an aromatic, nutty and peppery flavor. As with all seeds, herbs, and spices, cumin should be stored in a cool, dark place, where it will keep for up to 6 months.

noodles with toasted **wheat germ**

Makes 4 servings

As a child, I feasted on Grandma's tender homemade noodles simply tossed with butter and bread crumbs. The Italians are known for a similar recipe called Spaghetti con Sabbia (Spaghetti with Sand). These days my son often requests my version made with toasted wheat germ for extra nourishment.—Trust me, there are never any leftovers!

4 ounces spinach ribbon noodles
(about 2 cups)

4 ounces medium egg noodles
(about 2 cups)

1/4 cup butter

1/2 cup toasted wheat germ (see Tip)

1/2 teaspoon pepper, or to taste

Dash of salt, or to taste

3 plum tomatoes (at room temperature),
sliced

GARNISH (OPTIONAL) sprigs of fresh flat-leaf parsley

1. Bring a large pot of water to a boil over high heat; add salt, then the spinach and egg noodles. When the water returns to a boil, stir occasionally to separate the noodles. Reduce the heat to medium-high and cook for about 5 to 7 minutes, or according to package instructions, until noodles are *al dente*. Drain well; set aside and cover to keep warm.

2. Melt the butter in the pot over medium-high heat. Add the noodles and stir gently for about 3 minutes or until evenly coated. Toss in the wheat germ, pepper, and salt. Adjust the seasonings to taste.

3. Top each serving with tomato slices.

PER SERVING: Cal 332/Prot 10.5g/Carb 40.9g/Fat 14g/Chol 53mg/Sod 159mg

Noodle Frittata
(page 56)

noodle
frittata

Makes 4 servings

Frittatas are to Italians what omelets are to the French. The difference is that in a frittata the filling is combined with the eggs, and the whole mixture is cooked together and left flat rather than folded. Enjoy this frittata with fruit for breakfast or brunch; for lunch or dinner, serve it with your favorite tomato sauce and a side of steamed vegetables, such as asparagus spears or broccoli florets.

1/2 cup fine egg noodles (about 1 ounce)	Dash of salt
6 eggs	1 tablespoon olive oil
3 tablespoons cold water	1/4 cup finely chopped onion
1/2 cup freshly grated Romano cheese, divided (see Tip)	1/2 teaspoon minced garlic
1 teaspoon herbes de Provence (see Tip)	2 cups sliced cremini mushrooms (see Tip)
1/4 teaspoon pepper	1 tomato, cut into thin slices

GARNISH (OPTIONAL)   freshly ground black pepper, sprigs of fresh basil

1. Bring a small pot of water to a boil over high heat; add salt, then the noodles. When the water returns to a boil, stir occasionally to separate the noodles. Reduce the heat to medium-high and cook for about 3 to 5 minutes, or according to package instructions, until noodles are *al dente*. Drain well; rinse with cool water and drain again.

2. While the noodles are cooking, whisk the eggs lightly in a small bowl. Add the water and whisk again. Whisk in 1/4 cup of the cheese, herbes de Provence, pepper, salt, and noodles. Set aside.

3. Heat the oil in a large nonstick skillet over medium-high heat. Add the onion and garlic; cook, stirring constantly, for about 3 minutes or until tender but not browned. Add the mushrooms; cook, stirring occasionally, for about 2 minutes or until the mushrooms are tender. Reduce the heat to medium; pour the egg mixture into the pan. Stir gently until the eggs start to thicken; smooth the top surface with a spoon. As the egg mixture continues to cook, lift the edges with a fork to let the uncooked portion run underneath. When no visible liquid remains, about 2 minutes, arrange the tomato slices on the top of the frittata and sprinkle with the remaining 1/4 cup of the cheese. Cover and continue cooking for about 1 more minute or until the cheese is melted and the bottom of the frittata is lightly browned.

4. Cut into wedges for serving.

PER SERVING: Cal 241/Prot 16.6g/Carb 9.7g/Fat 15.1g/Chol 335mg/Sod 368mg

Variation

• Substitute 1^1/$_2$ cups cholesterol-free egg substitute for the eggs; omit the water.

> ## TIPS
>
> • Romano cheese is curded and aged the same way as Parmesan, except that it is made from sheep's milk rather than cow's milk. This gives it a sharper, more tangy flavor with less sweetness.
>
> • Herbes de Provence is a mixture of dried herbs commonly containing basil, fennel seed, lavender, marjoram, rosemary, sage, summer savory, and thyme. The blend can be found in small clay crocks in gourmet shops and some supermarkets; it is most often imported from the south of France, where it is a traditional flavoring.
>
> • The readily available cultivated white mushroom has a mild, earthy flavored; those labeled "button mushrooms" are immature, smaller white mushrooms. Cremini mushrooms (sometimes labeled "Italian brown mushrooms") are more flavorful, with a denser, less watery texture than white mushrooms; portobello mushrooms are larger, matured creminis

egg noodles and vegetables in spicy peanut sauce

Makes 4 servings

This meal can be prepared in less than 10 minutes using containers from your refrigerator and pantry and the odds and ends of nearly any vegetables you have on hand. Sometimes I make more than I'll need for dinner because this dish is just as satisfying the next day as a chilled noodle salad.

8 ounces wide egg noodles (about 4 cups)

4 cups broccoli florets

4 carrots, diagonally cut into 1/4-inch-thick slices (about 2 cups)

Spicy Peanut Sauce

1/3 cup hoisin sauce (see Tip)

1/3 cup nonfat plain yogurt (see Tip)

2 tablespoons smooth peanut butter

2 tablespoons low-sodium soy sauce

2 teaspoons chili paste with garlic, or to taste

1 teaspoon dark sesame oil

1/4 cup water, or as needed

To Complete the Recipe

2 medium scallions, coarsely chopped

GARNISH (OPTIONAL)   toasted sesame seeds

1. Bring a large pot of water to a boil over high heat; add salt, then the noodles. When the water returns to a boil, stir occasionally to separate the noodles. Reduce the heat to medium-high and cook for about 6 to 8 minutes, or according to package instructions, until noodles are *al dente*.

2. While the noodles are cooking, put the broccoli and carrots into a large microwave-proof dish. Add about ¼ cup water; cover and microwave on high for about 6 minutes or until crisp-tender. (Or cook the broccoli and carrots for about 6 minutes in a stove-top steamer.)

3. Meanwhile, whisk together the sauce ingredients in a small bowl. The sauce should have a cake-batter consistency; add the water as needed. Adjust the seasoning to taste.

4. When the noodles are done, drain well; return to the pot. Add the scallions, broccoli, and carrots; toss. Add the sauce; toss over medium heat just until heated through.

PER SERVING: Cal 415/Prot 16.4g/Carb 67.9g/Fat 8.7g/Chol 56mg/Sod 1039mg

ADVANCE PREPARATION   Covered and refrigerated, the sauce will keep for up to 3 days. Bring to room temperature or heat gently before tossing with hot, freshly cooked noodles and vegetables. The completed dish will keep up to 2 days.

Variation

• Substitute other vegetables for the broccoli and carrots (up to 6 cups total). Try steamed zucchini strips, blanched stemmed snap peas, or diced red bell pepper.

> ## TIPS
>
> • Hoisin sauce is a thick, sweet, reddish-brown sauce made from soybeans, sugar, chilies, spices, and garlic. It is sold in bottles in specialty Asian markets and in many supermarkets. Tightly sealed and refrigerated, it will keep almost indefinitely. If necessary, Chinese barbecue sauce can be used as a substitute.
>
> • Check the expiration date when buying yogurt; if refrigerated, it will keep for up to 1 week beyond that date. The watery layer in yogurt cartons is simply the whey rising to the top. Stir it back in; it has nothing to do with the age or quality of the yogurt.

curried vegetables

and egg noodle toss

Makes 4 servings

This recipe is adapted from my Chicken Curry recipe in The 15-Minute Gourmet: Chicken. *To add chicken, cut 8 ounces of boneless, skinless chicken breasts into 2-inch-long by $^1/_2$-inch-wide strips; cook in 1 tablespoon canola or safflower oil for about 5 to 6 minutes or until lightly browned and cooked through. Toss into the completed dish just before serving.*

8 ounces wide egg noodles (about 4 cups)

1 cup broccoli florets

2 carrots, diagonally cut into $^1/_4$-inch-thick slices

1 small onion, cut into $^1/_4$-inch-thick wedges (about 1 cup)

Curry Sauce

2 tablespoons cold water

1 tablespoon cornstarch

1 tablespoon canola or safflower oil

1 tablespoon curry powder, or to taste (see Tip)

1 tablespoon minced jalapeño pepper (or $^1/_4$ teaspoon red pepper flakes), or to taste

2 teaspoons finely minced fresh ginger

1 teaspoon minced garlic

$1^1/_4$ cups water

$^1/_2$ cup golden raisins

1 tablespoon fresh lime juice

$^1/_2$ teaspoon salt, or to taste

To Complete the Recipe

1 cup frozen baby peas, thawed

2 plum tomatoes, each cut into 8 wedges

$^1/_2$ cup raw cashews

GARNISH (OPTIONAL)   toasted sesame seeds

1. Bring a large pot of water to a boil over high heat; add salt, then the noodles. When the water returns to a boil, stir occasionally to separate the noodles. Reduce the heat to medium-high and cook for about 6 to 8 minutes, or according to package instructions, until noodles are *al dente*.

2. Meanwhile, put the broccoli, carrots, and onion in a medium microwave-proof dish; add about ¼ cup water. Cover and microwave on high for about 6 minutes or until tender. (Or cook the vegetables for about 6 minutes in a stovetop steamer.)

3. To prepare the Curry Sauce: Stir together the cold water and corn-starch in a small bowl until smooth; set aside. Heat the oil in a large nonstick sauté pan over medium-high heat. Add the curry powder, jalapeño pepper (if using), ginger, and garlic; stir constantly for about 1 minute or until fragrant. Stir in the water and raisins; cover and cook for about 3 minutes or until the raisins are softened and plumped. Reduce the heat to medium and add the water-corn-starch mixture; stir constantly for about 1 minute or until the sauce thickens slightly. Reduce the heat to low; stir in the lime juice, salt, and red pepper flakes (if using).

4. When the vegetables and noodles are done, drain well.

5. Stir the microwaved vegetables, peas, plum tomatoes, and cashews into the sauce. Add the noodles and stir gently until heated through.

> **TIP**
>
> Curry powder, a combination of many herbs and spices, is blended in literally thousands of versions. Domestic curry powders are usually quite mild. Imported brands often are more flavorful; some provide several choices labeled mild, medium, or hot. Since curry powder quickly loses its pungency, store it, airtight in a dark, dry place, for up to 3 months.

PER SERVING: Cal 510/Prot 16g/Carb 76.9g/Fat 15.8g/Chol 56mg/Sod 352mg

linguine with chicken
in creamy
peanut sauce

Makes 4 servings

Warning: This addictive sauce will tempt you to chase every last drop around the dish. Serve it with steamed dark green broccoli florets to add color and crunch.

12 ounces linguine

Creamy Peanut Sauce

1 tablespoon cold water

1 tablespoon cornstarch

1 (14$1/2$-ounce) can fat-free low-sodium chicken broth

$1/4$ cup smooth peanut butter (see Tip)

2 tablespoons low-sodium soy sauce

$1/2$ teaspoon dark sesame oil

$1/4$ teaspoon red pepper flakes, or to taste

To Complete the Recipe

1 tablespoon canola or safflower oil

1 medium onion, cut into $1/4$-inch-wide strips

1 red bell pepper, cut into $1/4$-inch-wide lengthwise strips

1 teaspoon minced garlic

1 teaspoon minced fresh ginger

12 ounces boneless skinless chicken breast halves, cut into 2-inch-long by $1/2$-inch-wide strips

Dash of salt, or to taste

GARNISH (OPTIONAL)   coarsely chopped scallions

1. Bring a large pot of water to a boil over high heat; add salt, then the linguine. When the water returns to a boil, stir occasionally to separate the linguine. Reduce the heat to

medium-high and cook for about 10 to 12 minutes, or according to package instructions, until noodles are *al dente*.

2. While the linguine is cooking, prepare the sauce: Stir together the cold water and cornstarch in a measuring cup until smooth. Combine the chicken broth, peanut butter, soy sauce, and sesame oil in a food processor; process until smooth. Transfer to a small bowl; whisk in the water-cornstarch mixture and red pepper flakes. Set aside.

3. Heat the canola or safflower oil in a large nonstick skillet over medium-high heat. Add the onion, bell pepper, garlic, and ginger; cook, stirring occasionally, for about 4 minutes or until the bell pepper is crisp-tender. Add the chicken; continue cooking, stirring occasionally, for about 5 to 6 more minutes or until the chicken is lightly browned and cooked through and the vegetables are tender.

4. Reduce the heat to medium; pour the sauce into the skillet. Cook, stirring constantly, for about 2 minutes or until it is thick and bubbly. Adjust the seasoning to taste.

5. When the linguine is done, drain well. Spoon the chicken and sauce over the linguine in individual pasta bowls.

> **TIP**
>
> Buy pure natural peanut butter with the oil on top; stir the oil back in before using. Many processed peanut butters are hydrogenated to prevent separation and have sugars, salt, and stabilizers added.

chapter 1 *Warm Noodles*

PER SERVING: Cal 621/Prot 45.5g/Carb 74.7g/Fat 15.6g/Chol 65mg/Sod 1390mg

five-spice shrimp
with plum sauce
over **noodles**

Makes 4 servings

The complex flavor of Chinese five-spice powder and the sweet-sour taste of plum sauce combine beautifully in this memorable dish.

1/2 cup Chinese plum sauce

1/4 cup water, or as needed

8 ounces thin Chinese wheat-flour noodles

1 tablespoon canola or safflower oil

4 ribs bok choy, diagonally cut into 1/4-inch-thick slices; also shred green tops (see Tip)

1/2 cup minced red bell pepper

2 medium scallions, finely chopped

1 teaspoon minced garlic

8 ounces medium shrimp (about 20), shelled and deveined

1 teaspoon five-spice powder (see Tip)

GARNISH (OPTIONAL)   toasted pine nuts

1. Bring a large pot of water to a boil over high heat.

2. Meanwhile, spoon the plum sauce into a small bowl. Stir in water, as needed, to reach a maple-syrup consistency. Set aside.

3. When the water comes to a boil, add the noodles. When the water returns to a boil, stir occasionally to separate the noodles. Reduce the heat to medium-high and cook for about 3 to 5 minutes, or according to package instructions, until noodles are *al dente*. When the noodles are done, drain well. Return to the pot and toss with about half of the sauce. Cover to keep warm.

4. Heat the oil in a large nonstick skillet over medium-high heat. Add the bok choy and greens, bell pepper, scallions, and garlic; cook, stirring occasionally, for about 3 minutes or until the vegetables are crisp-tender. Add the shrimp and five-spice powder; cook, stirring constantly, for about 2 to 3 minutes or until the shrimp are cooked through. (Be careful not to overcook.)

5. To serve, use tongs to transfer the noodles to pasta bowls; top with the shrimp-vegetable mixture. Drizzle with the remaining sauce.

   PER SERVING: Cal 334/Prot 17.2g/Carb 53.9g/Fat 5.5g/Chol 87mg/Sod 797mg

TIPS

- Bok choy should have unwilted dark-green leaves attached to firm light-green or white unblemished stalks; both the leaves and stalks are edible raw or cooked. Store bok choy in a plastic bag in the refrigerator for up to 3 days.

- Chinese five-spice powder, sometimes called five-fragrance powder, is a sweet and pungent mixture of five ground spices including fennel, star anise, Szechuan peppercorns, cinnamon, and cloves. A licorice flavor predominates, thanks to the fennel seeds. Some brands also contain ginger and licorice root. It is available in the ethnic section of most supermarkets and in Asian markets.

sherried
chicken-soba
stir-fry

Makes 4 servings

Sherry and hoisin sauce create a delectable blend of flavors that lend an enticing aroma as this dish cooks. With protein, starch, and vegetables all together, this is one-dish weeknight dining at its best—with a touch of elegance, too.

4 ounces soba noodles

Sherry-Hoisin Sauce

$1/4$ cup low-sodium soy sauce

$1/4$ cup dry sherry

2 tablespoons hoisin sauce

2 teaspoons sugar

To Complete the Recipe

2 tablespoons canola or safflower oil, divided

8 ounces boneless skinless chicken breast halves, cut into 2-inch-long by $1/2$-inch-wide strips

1 small onion, cut into $1/4$-inch-wide strips (about 1 cup)

2 carrots, diagonally cut into $1/8$-inch-thick slices

1 tablespoon minced fresh ginger

1 teaspoon minced garlic

4 cups coarsely shredded Chinese cabbage

1. Bring a medium pot of water to a boil over high heat; add the noodles. When the water returns to a boil, stir occasionally to separate the noodles. Reduce the heat to medium-high and cook for about 6 to 8 minutes, or according to package instructions, until noodles are *al dente*.

2. While the noodles are cooking, combine the sauce ingredients in a small bowl; stir until the sugar is dissolved. Set aside.

3. Heat 1 tablespoon of the oil in a large nonstick sauté pan over medium-high heat. Add the chicken; cook, stirring occasionally for about 5 to 6 minutes or until it is lightly browned and cooked through. Use a slotted spoon to transfer the chicken to a plate; cover to keep warm.

4. When the noodles are done, drain well; cover and set aside.

5. Heat the remaining 1 tablespoon of oil in the sauté pan over medium-high heat. Add the onion, carrots, ginger, and garlic; cook, stirring constantly, for about 2 minutes or until the carrots are crisp-tender. Add the cabbage and continue cooking, stirring constantly, for about 2 more minutes or until it is wilted. Reduce the heat to medium; stir in the chicken, sauce, and the noodles. Stir gently until the chicken and noodles are warmed through.

PER SERVING: Cal 347/Prot 25.3g/Carb 39.7g/Fat 9.7g/Chol 44mg/Sod 1199mg

TIPS

- Sautéing and stir-frying are similar cooking procedures. In sautéing, the food is stirred frequently. In stir-frying, the food is moved around constantly, producing foods with a more crisp-tender texture than those sautéed. For low-fat cooking, both procedures can be done with a small amount of oil, or even stock.

- You don't need a wok to stir-fry; a large sauté pan or skillet will do. Always begin with the firmest vegetables (such as broccoli, carrots, and cauliflower) and add the softest vegetables (such as zucchini and mushrooms) last. Do not cover the pan or the vegetables will lose their crispness.

pad
thai

Makes 4 servings

This is Thailand's best-known noodle dish, with as many variations as there are turkey stuffings in the United States. Traditionally, it is made using wide flat rice noodles. If there's no time for a trip to the Asian market and your supermarket does not carry them, substitute 8 ounces of fettucine, thin spaghetti, or lo mein noodles. For variety, add cooked shrimp or chicken strips when stirring the completed dish

6 ounces flat rice noodles (rice sticks)

Spicy Oyster Sauce

1 tablespoon cold water

2 teaspoons cornstarch

$3/4$ cup fat-free low-sodium chicken broth

2 tablespoons sugar

2 tablespoons oyster sauce (see Tip)

1 tablespoon low-sodium soy sauce

1 tablespoon Worcestershire sauce

1 tablespoon fresh lime juice

1 teaspoon minced fresh ginger

$1/4$ teaspoon chili powder

$1/4$ teaspoon red pepper flakes, or to taste

Dash of salt, or to taste

To Complete the Recipe

3 eggs

2 tablespoons cold water

1 tablespoon canola or safflower oil

1 cup coarsely chopped red bell pepper

1 small onion, cut into $1/4$-inch-wide strips (about 1 cup)

1 teaspoon minced garlic

1 cup fresh bean sprouts

GARNISH (OPTIONAL)   finely chopped unsalted dry-roasted peanuts, lime wedges, coarsely chopped fresh cilantro

1. Bring a large pot of water to a boil over high heat. Add the noodles; cook for about 3 to 5 minutes, or according to package instructions, until noodles are *al dente*. Stir occasionally to separate the noodles as they soften. Drain the noodles in a colander and rinse with cold water. Use kitchen shears to cut the noodles into shorter lengths, about 6 inches long; set aside.

2. Stir together the cold water and cornstarch in a small nonstick saucepan until smooth. Stir in the remaining sauce ingredients. Cook over medium heat, stirring occasionally, for about 4 minutes or until the sauce thickens to maple-syrup consistency. Remove from the heat, cover, and set aside.

3. While the sauce is cooking, whisk the eggs in a small bowl; add the water. Set aside.

4. Heat the oil in a large nonstick sauté pan over medium-high heat. Add the bell pepper, onion, and garlic; cook, stirring constantly, for about 3 minutes or until crisp-tender. Add the eggs; continue cooking, stirring constantly, for about 1 minute or until the onion is tender and the eggs are cooked through. Remove from the heat.

5. Immerse the cooked noodles in a pan of cold water; swirl them with your hand to separate. Without draining in a colander, lift handfuls of the noodles from the bowl; let drain slightly, then transfer them to the sauté pan.

6. Add the bean sprouts and sauce to the sauté pan; stir the mixture gently over medium heat just until heated through. Adjust the seasonings to taste.

> **TIP**
>
> Oyster sauce is a dark brown sauce made from oysters, brine, and soy sauce that have been cooked until thick and concentrated. Select a good quality brand with a thick consistency. It is available in many supermarkets and in all Asian markets. A vegetarian substitute, made from mushrooms and soybeans, is available in many Asian markets.

PER SERVING: Cal 329/Prot 10.4g/Carb 55.2g/Fat 7.4g/Chol 160mg/Sod 591mg

chinese **mapo tofu**
with wheat-flour noodles

Makes 4 servings

According to Nathan Fong, my culinary friend from Vancouver, B.C., Mapo Tofu means Grandmother's Tofu—and nearly every Chinese grandmother has her own version. Making this adaptation of his recipe takes only minutes, since it is prepared from ingredients in your pantry. You can adjust the hotness to suit your taste.

1 tablespoon canola or safflower oil

1/2 cup finely chopped onion

2 teaspoons minced jalapeño pepper

1 teaspoon minced garlic

1/2 cup fat-free low-sodium chicken broth

1/4 cup oyster sauce

2 tablespoons low-sodium soy sauce

1 tablespoon dark sesame oil (see Tip)

1 teaspoon sugar

1/8 teaspoon red pepper flakes, optional

12 ounces silken extra-firm tofu, cut into 1/2-inch cubes (about 2 cups); (see Tip)

1 cup frozen baby peas, thawed

4 ounces thin Chinese wheat-flour noodles

2 tablespoons minced fresh cilantro

GARNISH (OPTIONAL) finely chopped scallions

1. Bring a large pot of water to a boil over high heat.

2. Meanwhile, heat the oil in a large nonstick sauté pan over medium-high heat. Add the onion, jalapeño pepper, and garlic; cook, stirring occasionally, for about 3 minutes or until the onion is crisp-tender.

3. Combine the chicken broth, oyster sauce, soy sauce, sesame oil, sugar, and red pepper flakes in a small bowl.

4. Add the chicken broth mixture to the sauté pan. Cook, stirring occasionally, for about 2 minutes or until the onion is tender and the sauce is slightly reduced.

5. Meanwhile, add the noodles to the pot of boiling water. When the water returns to a boil, stir occasionally to separate the noodles. Reduce the heat to medium-high and cook for about 3 to 5 minutes, or according to package instructions, until noodles are *al dente*. Drain well.

6. Reduce the heat to medium; gently stir the tofu and peas into the sauté pan. Cover for about 1 minute or until the tofu is heated through. Add the noodles and cilantro; toss gently.

PER SERVING: Cal 273/Prot 13.1g/Carb 33.8g/Fat 9.5g/Chol 0mg/Sod 1073mg

TIPS

- Buy dark, amber-colored sesame oil, made from toasted sesame seeds, rather than light-colored sesame oil. The light oils are extracted from raw sesame seeds and lack the distinctive strong flavor. Because dark sesame oil is so volatile, it is used as a flavoring oil rather than as a cooking oil and is usually added as one of the last steps in a cooked recipe.

- Tofu is made from soybeans, through a process that resembles cheese making. The curds are pressed into blocks labeled soft, medium, firm, and extra-firm, depending on how much water was released. Soft and medium tofu can be blended to a smooth, creamy consistency and are the best choice for making dressings and sauces; firm and extra-firm tofu have a denser consistency and hold their shape when cut into cubes. "Silken" tofu has a mild flavor and smooth texture. For more information on tofu and soy products and more tofu recipes, see my cookbook *The Complete Soy Cookbook.*

stir-fried
rice noodles
with **prawns**

Makes 4 servings

My friend Nathan Fong sometimes adds Chinese barbecued pork to this recipe. If that suits you too, julienne about $^1/_2$ pound of the ready-to-serve pork that is available in most Asian markets; add it along with the bean sprouts and stir gently until it is heated through.

8 ounces flat rice noodles (rice sticks)

Oyster-Sesame Sauce

$^1/_4$ cup oyster sauce

$^1/_4$ cup low-sodium soy sauce

2 tablespoons white rice vinegar

2 teaspoons dark sesame oil

1 teaspoon chili paste with garlic, or to taste

$^1/_2$ teaspoon salt, or to taste (see Tip)

To Complete the Recipe

2 tablespoons canola or safflower oil

1 cup onion in $^1/_4$-inch-wide strips

4 medium scallions, cut into 1-inch-long pieces

2 teaspoons minced fresh ginger

1 teaspoon minced garlic

8 ounces medium shrimp (about 20), shelled and deveined

4 cups fresh bean sprouts

1. Bring a large pot of water to a boil over high heat. Add the noodles; cook for about 3 to 5 minutes, or according to package instructions, until noodles are *al dente*. Stir occasionally to separate the noodles as they soften. Drain the noodles in a colander and rinse with cold water. Use kitchen shears to cut the noodles into shorter lengths, about 6 inches long; set aside.

2. Meanwhile, stir together the sauce ingredients in a medium bowl; set aside.

3. Heat the canola or safflower oil in a large nonstick sauté pan over medium-high heat. Add the onion, scallions, ginger, and garlic; cook, stirring occasionally, for about 3 minutes or until the onion is crisp-tender. Add the shrimp; cook, stirring constantly, for about 2 to 3 minutes or until they are cooked through. Remove from the heat.

4. Immerse the cooked noodles in a pan of cold water; swirl them with your hand to separate. Without draining in a colander, lift handfuls of the noodles from the bowl; let drain slightly, then transfer them to the sauté pan. Add the bean sprouts and the sauce. Stir gently over medium heat just until heated through. Adjust the seasonings to taste.

PER SERVING: Cal 419/Prot 19.8g/Carb 61.3g/Fat 10.5g/Chol 87mg/Sod 1215mg

> ### TIP
>
> Sea salt, available in many supermarkets as well as health food stores, is generally obtained by evaporating sea water in enclosed, protected bays. The salt is purified during this process, leaving a salt with a high percentage of sodium chloride and many trace elements, including magnesium, zinc, calcium, iron, and potassium. Because of its fuller flavor, less is usually needed. Fine sea salt can be used just like ordinary table salt. Coarse crystals are used to salt cooking water. The crystals can be finely ground in a salt mill for use in recipes or at the table.

chapter 1 *Warm Noodles*

lo mein
with thai
coconut-peanut sauce

Makes 4 servings

Be sure to use pure natural peanut butter without added sugar. Then make this creamy sauce mildly spicy or decidedly zesty, depending on the amount of red pepper flakes you choose to add.

8 ounces lo mein noodles

Thai Coconut-Peanut Sauce

1 cup canned low-fat coconut milk (see Tip)

1/2 cup smooth peanut butter

2 teaspoons minced garlic

1/2 teaspoon red pepper flakes, or to taste

Dash of salt, or to taste

1/4 cup fresh lime juice

Water, as needed

To Complete the Recipe

1 cup stemmed snow peas, blanched (see Tip)

1/2 cup minced red bell pepper

2 medium scallions, coarsely chopped

1/4 cup chopped fresh cilantro, or to taste

GARNISH (OPTIONAL)   finely chopped unsalted dry-roasted peanuts, lime wedges, sprigs of fresh cilantro

1. Bring a large pot of water to a boil over high heat; add the noodles. When the water returns to a boil, stir occasionally to separate the noodles. Reduce the heat to medium-high and cook for about 3 to 4 minutes, or according to package instructions, until noodles are *al dente*.

2. While the noodles are cooking, combine the coconut milk, peanut butter, garlic, red pepper flakes, and salt in a medium nonstick saucepan over medium heat; stir until the sauce is creamy and smooth. Remove from the heat; stir in the lime juice. The sauce should have a cake-batter consistency; add water, as needed.

3. When the noodles are done, drain well; return to the pot. Add the peanut sauce and toss. Add the remaining ingredients; toss over medium heat just until heated through. Adjust the seasonings to taste.

   PER SERVING: Cal 475/Prot 16mg/Carb 60mg/Fat 22.2mg/Chol 0mg/Sod 66mg

Variation

*   Substitute steamed broccoli florets for the blanched snow peas.

TIPS

*   Do not confuse canned unsweetened coconut milk with "cream of coconut," used mainly for desserts and mixed drinks. Low-fat, or "lite," coconut milk, available in health food stores, Asian markets, and some supermarkets, contains about half the calories and fat of regular coconut milk. In both products, the coconut fat naturally separates from the coconut milk; shake well before using. Leftover coconut milk can be frozen.

*   Snow peas, or Chinese snow peas, have edible pods containing tender and sweet seeds. Choose thin, bright green pods with small seeds. Refrigerate in a plastic bag for up to 3 days. Just before using, pinch off both tips and remove the tough strings from the inner curve of the more mature pods.

East Indian Noodles with Split Peas and Cashews

east indian
noodles with **split peas**
and cashews

Makes 4 servings

The day my friend Raghavan Iyer shared this traditional East Indian recipe with me, he taught me how to heat the mustard seeds until they pop, filling my kitchen with an enticing aroma. For lunch we feasted on this colorful dish that unites a fascinating blend of flavors and textures, including the intrigue of slightly crunchy split peas and raw cashews. The fresh curry leaves lend a distinctive flavor; but if they are unavailable, add more cilantro. Traditionally this is a vegetarian dish, but you can toss in cooked shrimp along with the noodles if you wish.

8 ounces flat rice noodles (rice sticks)

1 tablespoon canola or safflower oil

1 teaspoon brown or yellow mustard seeds (see Tip)

1 cup red onion in $1/4$-inch-wide strips

$1/4$ cup dried yellow split peas (see Tip)

$1/2$ cup raw cashews

1 (10-ounce) package frozen chopped spinach, thawed (do not drain liquid)

1 red bell pepper, cut into $1/4$-inch-wide lengthwise strips

$1/3$ cup fresh lime juice

$1/4$ cup chopped fresh cilantro

2 green Thai chilies, finely chopped, include seeds, or to taste (see Tip)

8 to 10 whole fresh curry leaves (see Tip)

$1/2$ teaspoon salt, or to taste

$1/2$ teaspoon ground turmeric

1. Bring a large pot of water to a boil over high heat. Add the noodles; cook for about 3 to 5 minutes, or according to package instructions, until noodles are *al dente*. Stir occasionally to separate the noodles as they soften. Drain the noodles in a colander and rinse with cold water. Use kitchen shears to cut the noodles into shorter lengths, about 6 inches long; set aside.

(continues)

2. While the noodles are cooling, heat the oil in a large nonstick sauté pan over medium-high heat. Add the mustard seeds; cover and heat for about 30 seconds or until they stop popping. Reduce the heat to medium-high and add the onion; cook, stirring constantly, for about 2 minutes or until it is crisp-tender. Add the split peas and cashews; cook, stirring constantly, for about 2 minutes or until they are golden brown. Add the spinach with its liquid and the bell pepper; stir for about 2 minutes or until the bell pepper is crisp-tender. Remove the pan from the heat. Stir in the lime juice, cilantro, chilies, curry leaves, salt, and turmeric.

3. Immerse the cooked noodles in a pan of cold water; swirl them with your hand to separate. Without draining in a colander, transfer handfuls of the noodles, with whatever water that clings to them, to the sauté pan. Stir the mixture gently over medium-high heat just until heated through. Adjust the seasonings to taste.

4. Serve with the whole curry leaves in the dish, but they are not meant to be eaten.

PER SERVING: Cal 441/Prot 12.3g/Carb 69.8g/Fat 12.6g/Chol 0mg/Sod 334mg

Variation

*   Substitute jalapeño peppers or serrano peppers for the green Thai chilies.

TIPS

*   Whole mustard seeds are available in the spice section of most supermarkets. Compared with the yellow (or white) seeds, the brown (or Asian) seeds are smaller but more pungent in flavor. Store the seeds for up to 1 year in a dark, dry place.

*   Split peas, both yellow and green, are grown for drying. In the process, they are split along a natural seam, which explains their name. The peas are available in supermarkets and health food stores. They will keep indefinitely if stored in a tightly closed container in a cool, dry place. The flavors differ, so yellow and green split peas are not interchangeable in recipes.

*   Thai chilies are about 1 to 1$^1/_2$ inches long and just $^1/_4$ inch in diameter; they range in color from green to red when fully ripe. Their fiery flavor does not dissipate with cooking. For a milder flavor, remove and discard the seeds before chopping the chilies.

*   Curry leaves which look like shiny lemon leaves, are available in Indian and Asian markets. They have a curry fragrance and a flavor that is essential to many East Indian dishes. Refrigerate them in an airtight container for up to 2 weeks or freeze them for up to 2 months. Packaged dried curry leaves can be substituted but are less flavorful.

asian noodles with
black bean-
peanut sauce

Makes 4 servings

On its own, the flavor of Asian black bean sauce can be quite intense; but when it is combined with other ingredients, the blend makes a delicious complement to noodles and crisp-tender vegetables.

Black Bean–Peanut Sauce

$^1/_2$ cup finely chopped unsalted dry-
    roasted peanuts

$^1/_4$ cup oyster sauce

3 tablespoons Asian black bean sauce
    (see Tip)

2 tablespoons white rice vinegar

To Complete the Recipe

1 tablespoon roasted peanut oil

1 small onion, halved and cut into
    $^1/_4$-inch-wide strips (about 1 cup)

2 cups stemmed snow pea strips (pods
    halved lengthwise)

1 red bell pepper, cut into $^1/_4$-inch-wide
    lengthwise strips

1 tablespoon minced garlic

8 ounces lo mein noodles

GARNISH (OPTIONAL)   sprigs of fresh cilantro

1. Bring a large pot of water to a boil over high heat.

2. Meanwhile, stir together the sauce ingredients in a small bowl; set aside.

(continues)

79

3. Heat the oil in a large nonstick skillet over medium-high heat. Add the onion; cook, stirring constantly for about 2 minutes or until slightly tender. Add the snow peas, bell pepper, and garlic; continue to cook, stirring constantly, for about 5 more minutes or until the snow peas and bell pepper are crisp-tender. Reduce the heat to low.

4. While the vegetables are cooking, add the noodles to the pot of boiling water. When the water returns to a boil, stir occasionally to separate the noodles. Reduce the heat to medium-high and cook for about 3 to 4 minutes, or according to package instructions, until noodles are *al dente*. Drain well.

5. Return the noodles to the pot. Add the vegetables; toss over medium heat. Add the sauce and toss again just until heated through.

> ### TIP
>
> Asian black bean sauce is a salty purée of fermented black soy beans, sugar, salt, and garlic. It is found in Asian markets and in the Asian section of most supermarkets. Store, tightly covered, in the refrigerator for up to 1 year.

PER SERVING: Cal 419/Prot 11.7g/Carb 64.4g/Fat 12g/Chol 0mg/Sod 728mg

ADVANCE PREPARATION   Covered and refrigerated, the sauce will keep for several days. Bring to room temperature before tossing with hot, freshly cooked noodles and vegetables.

Variation

- Substitute other vegetables for the snow peas or bell pepper (up to 4 cups total). Try small broccoli florets or shredded carrots.

sesame-soy chicken
and crispy vegetables
with **ramen**

Makes 4 servings

This sweet and slightly spicy sauce is absolutely delicious warm, but the dish is equally as enticing chilled and served later as a noodle salad.

1 tablespoon canola or safflower oil

12 ounces boneless skinless chicken
breast halves, cut into 2-inch-long by
$1/2$-inch-wide strips

Dash of pepper

Sesame-Soy Sauce

3 tablespoons dark sesame oil

3 tablespoons low-sodium soy sauce

2 tablespoons dry sherry

2 tablespoons honey

Dash of ground allspice

Dash of red pepper flakes, or to taste

Dash of pepper, or to taste

Dash of salt, or to taste

To Complete the Recipe

6 ounces baked ramen noodles

$1/2$ cup coarsely shredded daikon radish
(see Tip)

$1/2$ cup coarsely shredded carrot

2 medium scallions, thinly sliced

GARNISH (OPTIONAL)   toasted sesame seeds

(continues)

1. Bring a medium pot of water to a boil over high heat.

2. Meanwhile, heat the canola or safflower oil in a large nonstick sauté pan over medium-high heat. Add the chicken; cook, stirring occasionally, for about 5 to 6 minutes or until it is lightly browned and cooked through.

TIP

Daikon is a large Asian radish, ranging in size from 6 to 15 inches in length and about 2 to 3 inches in diameter, although some are much thicker. The skin can be creamy white or black; the flesh inside is white with a crisp and juicy texture and a mild flavor. Wrap the radish in a plastic bag and refrigerate for up to 1 week. Daikons are used raw in salads or can be used as an ingredient in stir-fries; the flavor turns sweeter when cooked.

3. While the chicken is cooking, whisk together the sauce ingredients in a small bowl.

4. When the chicken is nearly done, drop the noodles into the boiling water. Reduce the heat to medium-high and cook for about 3 to 5 minutes, or according to package instructions, until noodles are *al dente*. As the noodles cook, stir occasionally with a fork to separate. Drain well.

5. Transfer the noodles to a large bowl. Add the radish, carrot, and scallions; toss. Add the sauce and toss.

6. When the chicken is done, sprinkle lightly with pepper. Add to the noodle mixture and toss again. Adjust the seasonings to taste.

PER SERVING: Cal 463/Prot 29.5g/Carb 47g/Fat 17.5g/Chol/ 65mg/Sod 674mg

asian
pasta primavera

Makes 4 servings

Euro-Asian fusion means cross-blending whatever works; so feel free to substitute linguine for the lo mein noodles and to add other vegetables, such as julienned carrots or thinly sliced bok choy, to cook with the ginger and garlic. To make a more substantial meal, top the servings with grilled or stir-fried large shrimp. I prepare a full recipe even when I need only two servings, because the chilled leftovers make a delectable lunch the next day.

Soy-Sesame Sauce

3 tablespoons low-sodium soy sauce

1 tablespoon dark sesame oil

1 tablespoon fresh lemon juice

Dash of ground white pepper, or to taste

To Complete the Recipe

1 tablespoon canola or safflower oil

1 teaspoon minced fresh ginger

1 teaspoon minced garlic

1 cup asparagus in 1-inch-long diagonally cut pieces

3 ounces stemmed shiitake mushrooms, caps cut into $1/2$-inch-wide slices (about 2 cups); (see Tips)

1 cup fresh bean sprouts

$1/2$ yellow bell pepper, cut into $1/4$-inch-wide lengthwise strips

2 medium scallions, diagonally cut into $1 1/2$-inch-long pieces

8 ounces lo mein noodles

GARNISH (OPTIONAL)   black sesame seeds or nori cut into julienne strips

1. Bring a large pot of water to a boil over high heat.

(continues)

2. Meanwhile, stir together the sauce ingredients; set aside.

3. Heat the canola or safflower oil in a large nonstick sauté pan over medium-high heat. Add the ginger and garlic; cook, stirring constantly, for about 30 seconds or until fragrant. Add the asparagus; cook, stirring constantly, for about 2 minutes or just until it begins to become crisp-tender. Add the mushrooms, bean sprouts, bell pepper, and scallions; continue to cook, stirring constantly, for about 4 more minutes or until the asparagus is crisp-tender. Remove from the heat.

4. While the vegetables are cooking, add the noodles to the pot of boiling water. When the water returns to a boil, stir occasionally to separate the noodles. Reduce the heat to medium-high and cook for about 3 to 4 minutes, or according to package instructions, until noodles are *al dente*. Drain well.

5. Return the noodles to the pot. Add the vegetables and soy sauce mixture; toss over medium heat just until heated through. Adjust the seasoning to taste.

PER SERVING: Cal 318/Prot 8.1g/Carb 55.3g/Fat 7.1g/Chol 0mg/Sod 432mg

Variation

• Substitute other vegetables for the asparagus or mushrooms (up to 4 cups total). Try small broccoli florets or red bell pepper strips.

TIPS

• Fresh shiitake mushrooms are large, umbrella-shaped mushrooms, brown-black in color, with a rich and unique flavor. Choose plump mushrooms with edges that turn under; avoid broken or shriveled caps. Store shiitake mushrooms in the refrigerator for up to 3 days, in a dish covered with a damp cloth or paper towel rather than in a closed container or plastic bag. The stems are extremely tough and should be removed. (You can use them to add flavor to stocks and sauces; discard the stems after they have been used for flavoring.)

• Dried shiitake mushrooms, sometimes called Chinese black mushrooms, can be stored at room temperature in a jar or sealed bag. To reconstitute before using in recipes, cover them with boiling water and soak for about 5 minutes, or until softened. As with fresh shiitake mushrooms, the stems are tough and must be removed.

Ramen, Asparagus, and Sherry-Orange Sauce
(page 86)

ramen, asparagus,
and sherry-orange sauce

Makes 4 servings

My son likes this dish served warm; I especially enjoy the leftovers for lunch the next day at room temperature or slightly chilled. Suit yourself.

Sherry-Orange Sauce

1 tablespoon cold water

1 teaspoon cornstarch

1/4 cup dry sherry (see Tip)

1/4 cup fresh orange juice

2 tablespoons low-sodium soy sauce

1 tablespoon dark sesame oil

1 tablespoon hoisin sauce

1/2 teaspoon chili paste with garlic, or to taste

Dash of ground white pepper, or to taste

To Complete the Recipe

1 tablespoon canola or safflower oil

2 cups asparagus diagonally cut into 2-inch-long pieces

1 red bell pepper, coarsely chopped

2 medium scallions, coarsely chopped

1 teaspoon minced garlic

6 ounces baked ramen noodles

GARNISH (OPTIONAL)   toasted sliced almonds or toasted sesame seeds, sprigs of fresh cilantro

1. Bring a medium pot of water to a boil over high heat.

2. Meanwhile, stir together the cold water and cornstarch in a small bowl until smooth. Whisk in the remaining sauce ingredients; set aside.

3. Heat the canola or safflower oil in a medium nonstick sauté pan over medium-high heat. Add the asparagus, bell pepper, scallions, and garlic; cook, stirring constantly, for about 5 minutes or until the asparagus is crisp-tender. Whisk the sauce and pour it into the skillet; stir constantly for about 1 minutes or until the mixture thickens to maple-syrup consistency. Remove from the heat; cover and set aside.

4. Drop the noodles into the boiling water. Reduce the heat to medium-high and cook for about 3 to 4 minutes, or according to package instructions, until noodles are *al dente*. As the noodles cook, stir occasionally with a fork to separate. Drain well.

5. Add the noodles to the sauté pan; toss the mixture over medium heat just until heated through. Adjust the seasonings to taste.

PER SERVING: Cal 282/Prot 7g/Carb 44.5g/Fat 8.4g/Chol 0mg/Sod 558mg

Variation

• Substitute thin Chinese wheat-flour noodles for the ramen noodles; cook according to package instructions.

> **TIP**
>
> Sherry is wine to which brandy has been added to increase the flavor and alcohol content. Sherries vary in color, flavor, and sweetness. Finos are dry and light; manzanillas are very dry, delicate finos, with a hint of saltiness. Olorosos, often labeled cream or golden sherry, are darker in color and sweet.

sesame soba noodles
with chinese
tahini sauce

Makes 4 servings

Tahini and chili paste with garlic are both highly flavored ingredients; put them together and the combination is magical, especially when paired with the distinctive earthiness of soba. Serve the dish warm. Refrigerate the leftovers, then bring them to room temperature the next day before eating.

8 ounces soba noodles

Chinese Tahini Sauce

2 tablespoons dark sesame oil

1 tablespoon tahini (see Tip)

1 tablespoon chili paste with garlic, or
   to taste (see Tip)

1 tablespoon low-sodium soy sauce

1 tablespoon white rice vinegar

1 teaspoon minced fresh ginger

2 teaspoons honey

1 tablespoon water, or as needed

To Complete the Recipe

1/2 cup minced red bell pepper

1 medium scallion, minced

1 tablespoon toasted sesame seeds

GARNISH (OPTIONAL)   sprigs of fresh cilantro

1. Bring a large pot of water to a boil over high heat; add the noodles. When the water returns to a boil, stir occasionally to separate the noodles. Reduce the heat

to medium-high and cook for about 6 to 8 minutes, or according to package instructions, until noodles are *al dente*.

2. While the noodles are cooking, whisk together the sauce ingredients in a small bowl. The sauce should have a cake-batter consistency; add the water as needed.

3. When the noodles are done, drain well; return to the pot. Add the bell pepper and scallion; toss. Add the sauce and toss again. Adjust the seasoning to taste.

PER SERVING: Cal 310/Prot 10.9g/Carb 42.2g/Fat 10.9g/Chol 0mg/Sod 837mg

TIPS

- Tahini, a paste made from ground sesame seeds, is also called sesame butter. Light tahini is preferable to the more intensely flavored dark tahini, which is made from toasted sesame seeds. Stir before using to reincorporate the oil. Keep tahini refrigerated in a tightly closed container for up to 1 year; bring to room temperature before using.

- Chili paste with garlic, also called chili purée or Chinese chili sauce, is found in Asian markets and in the Asian foods section of most supermarkets. Refrigerate it after opening.

vegetable **stir-fry**
with **ginger sauce**

Makes 4 servings

Consider this your basic stir-fry recipe and vary the vegetables to suit your taste or to use whatever you have on hand. Always begin by stir-frying the firmest vegetables first, so they will cook to the proper consistency.

Ginger Sauce

2 tablespoons cold water

1 tablespoon cornstarch (see Tip)

$1/3$ cup white rice vinegar

$1/3$ cup sugar

$1/2$ cup room temperature water

2 tablespoons low-sodium soy sauce

1 tablespoon finely minced fresh ginger

To Complete the Recipe

1 tablespoon canola or safflower oil

2 carrots, diagonally cut into $1/8$-inch-thick slices

1 small onion, thinly sliced (about 1 cup)

1 teaspoon minced garlic

4 ribs bok choy, diagonally cut into $1/2$-inch-thick slices; also shred green tops

$1 1/2$ cups sliced mushrooms

$1/2$ red bell pepper, cut into 2-inch-long by $1/4$-inch-wide strips

8 ounces thin Chinese wheat-flour noodles

GARNISH (OPTIONAL)   toasted sesame seeds

1. Bring a large pot of water to a boil over high heat.

2. Meanwhile, prepare the sauce: Stir together the cold water and cornstarch in a small bowl until smooth; set aside. Combine the vinegar, sugar, room temperature water, and soy sauce

in a small saucepan. Bring the mixture to a boil over medium-high heat, stirring occasionally for about 2 minutes or until the sugar is dissolved. Add the water-cornstarch mixture; stir constantly until the mixture is clear and thickened to maple-syrup consistency. Remove the pan from the heat; stir in the ginger. Set aside and cover to keep warm.

3. To stir-fry the vegetables, heat the oil in a large nonstick skillet over medium-high heat. Add the carrots and onion; cook, stirring constantly, for about 2 minutes. Add the remaining ingredients; continue to cook, stirring constantly, for about 4 more minutes or until the vegetables are crisp-tender.

4. While the vegetables are cooking, add the noodles to the pot of boiling water. When the water returns to a boil, stir occasionally to separate the noodles. Reduce the heat to medium-high and cook for about 3 to 5 minutes, or according to package instructions, until noodles are *al dente.* Drain well.

5. To serve, use tongs to transfer the noodles to shallow bowls or plates; top with the stir-fried vegetables and drizzle with Ginger Sauce.

PER SERVING: Cal 347/Prot 7.3g/Carb 68.8g/Fat 4.7g/Chol 0mg/Sod 966mg

ADVANCE PREPARATION   Covered and refrigerated, the sauce will keep for up to 2 days; reheat gently before serving. The vegetables can be chopped several hours in advance; stir-fry the vegetables, cook the noodles, and assemble the servings with the sauce just before serving.

> ## TIP
>
> Cornstarch, a fine white flour obtained from corn, is used as a thickener. It gives sauces a glossy, almost transparent look, rather than the cloudy appearance provided by flour thickening. Cornstarch works best when mixed with enough cold water to form a smooth, thin paste, which is then added to a hot mixture near the end of the cooking time. Stir constantly but gently as you add the water-cornstarch mixture; cook just long enough to thicken. Mixtures thickened with cornstarch will become thin if cooked too long, at too high a temperature, or if not stirred gently. Arrowroot, a fine powder made from a tropical tuber, can be substituted for cornstarch in equal amounts.

Variations

•   Add strips of chicken breast or shrimp: Stir-fry them first and remove them from the skillet with a slotted spoon; set aside and cover to keep warm. Add vegetables just before serving.

•   Substitute other vegetables for the carrots, bok choy, mushrooms, or red bell pepper, or add other vegetables (up to 4 to 6 cups total). Try broccoli florets, sliced zucchini, baby corn ears, sliced water chestnuts, fresh bean sprouts, snow peas, or frozen baby peas (thawed).

soba noodles with
chinese cabbage
and eggs

Makes 4 servings

Soba noodles mean comfort food to me. Here the eggs sauce the dish and blend well with the Asian flavors. Serve this to your family as a wholesome weeknight dinner. To add color to the plate, toss on some coarsely chopped steamed asparagus spears.

4 ounces soba noodles

4 eggs

2 tablespoons water

1 tablespoon canola or safflower oil

4 cups finely shredded Chinese cabbage

2 cups sliced mushrooms

2 medium scallions, finely chopped

1 rib celery, thinly sliced

1/4 cup diced red bell pepper

1 tablespoon low-sodium soy sauce, or to taste

1/4 teaspoon ground white pepper, or to taste (see Tip)

Dash of salt, or to taste

1. Bring a medium pot of water to a boil over high heat; add the noodles. When the water returns to a boil, stir occasionally to separate the noodles. Reduce the heat to medium-high and cook for about 6 to 8 minutes, or according to package instructions, until noodles are *al dente*.

2. Meanwhile, lightly whisk the eggs in a small bowl. Whisk in the water; set aside.

3. Heat the oil in a large nonstick skillet over medium-high heat. Add the cabbage, mushrooms, scallions, celery, and bell pepper; cook, stirring occasionally, for about 5 minutes or until the cabbage is wilted and the other vegetables are tender. Add the eggs; stir gently for about 1 minute or until they are nearly set. Remove from the heat.

4. When the noodles are done, drain well. Add them to the egg mixture; toss gently. Add the soy sauce, pepper, and salt; toss over medium heat just until the mixture is heated through. Adjust the seasonings to taste.

PER SERVING: Cal 232/Prot 13g/Carb 24.1g/Fat 9.3g/Chol 213mg/Sod 577mg

Variation

• Substitute 1 cup cholesterol-free egg substitute for the eggs; omit the water.

> ## TIP
>
> Berries of the pepper vine are used to produce both black pepper and white pepper. For black pepper, green berries are picked and sun-dried, turning black and shrinking in the process. For white pepper, the berries are allowed to ripen on the vine; they are picked and soaked in water to remove the outer coating, leaving the inner gray-white kernel. These inner kernels are sun-dried to produce white pepper. White pepper is slightly less spicy than black pepper. It is often used in Asian recipes and in light-colored sauces where dark specks of black pepper would stand out.

ginger
noodles

Makes 4 servings

For ginger lovers only! Thanks to lots of fresh fresh ginger, the flavor is assertive, making this dish ideal to serve in side portions to accompany broiled or grilled teriyaki-glazed salmon fillets. Thin Chinese wheat-flour noodles can be substituted for the egg noodles.

$1/3$ cup oyster sauce

2 tablespoons roasted peanut oil, divided

$1/8$ teaspoon pepper, or to taste

1 tablespoon water, or as needed

1 piece fresh ginger, about 4 inches long and 1 inch thick (about 2 ounces), peeled and cut into matchstick strips about $1^{1}/2$ inches long and $1/16$ inch thick (about $1/2$ cup); (see Tips)

6 medium scallions, cut into $1^{1}/2$-inch-long by $1/8$-inch-wide strips (about $1^{1}/2$ cups)

1 cup stemmed snow peas in $1/4$-inch-wide lengthwise strips

8 ounces thin Chinese egg noodles

GARNISH (OPTIONAL)   sprigs of fresh cilantro

1. Bring a large pot of unsalted water to a boil over high heat.

2. Meanwhile, stir together the oyster sauce, 1 tablespoon of the oil, and the pepper in a small bowl. Stir in water, as needed, to reach a cake-batter consistency; set aside.

3. Heat the remaining 1 tablespoon of the oil in a large nonstick sauté pan over medium-high heat. Add the ginger and cook, stirring constantly, for about 2 minutes or until it is aromatic and crisp-tender. Add the scallions and snow peas; cook, stirring constantly, for about 2 more minutes or until the fresh ginger, scallions, and snow peas are tender.

4. While the vegetables are cooking, add the noodles to the pot of boiling water. Reduce the heat to medium-high and cook for about 3 to 5 minutes, or according to package instructions, until noodles are *al dente*. As the noodles cook, stir occasionally with a fork to separate. Drain well.

5. Return the noodles to the pot. Add the scallion-snow pea mixture; toss over medium heat. Add the oyster sauce mixture and toss again just until heated through. Adjust the seasoning to taste.

PER SERVING: Cal 307/Prot 9.3g/Carb 49.8g/Fat 7.9g/Chol 0mg/Sod 413mg

TIPS

- Fresh ginger is available in 2 forms—young or mature. Young, or spring, ginger is found in Asian markets during the spring. It has pale, thin skin and requires no peeling. The texture is more tender and less fibrous, and the flavor is milder than its more mature form. When buying mature ginger, look for a piece that is firm, with smooth brown skin and no soft spots. Store at room temperature and use within a few days. Before using the ginger in recipes, peeling or not is optional. Finely mince the ginger so the flavor will be distributed evenly in the dish.

- Here are two ways to preserve ginger: Peel the fresh ginger and cut it into chunks; place in a jar and add sherry to cover. Cap the jar and refrigerate for up to 2 months. (The ginger won't absorb the flavor of the sherry.) For even longer storage, wrap the ginger tightly in aluminum foil or seal in a small zip-top plastic bag and freeze. When you need ginger, there's no need to thaw, simply use a fine grater to grate off the amount needed. Rewrap and replace immediately in the freezer. Frozen ginger will keep for up to 3 months.

- Jars of preminced ginger are available in most produce departments; check the labels, since some products also contain garlic and sweeteners. Dried ginger does not equate with fresh in Asian recipes.

chapter 2

Pestos, Salsas, and Fresh Sauces

TOSSING PESTOS, SALSAS, AND UNCOOKED SAUCES

with freshly cooked noodles is one of the best ways to get dinner on the table in a hurry. The secret to success is using fresh herbs and vegetables, high-quality oils and vinegars, and other flavorful ingredients, like garlic, ginger, sun-dried tomatoes, roasted red bell peppers, olives, and toasted nuts. In pestos, the ingredients are finely chopped

in a food processor to make a paste that may be either smooth or course in texture. In salsas, the components are stirred together and left chunky. Because their fresh, pungent flavors are in no way altered by the heat of cooking, the ingredients are at their best to wake up the palate. My uncooked sauces are made with ricotta cheese that is puréed until creamy, then gently heated before tossing with hot pasta.

Nearly all the recipes in this chapter can be made in advance and refrigerated; some can be frozen. When you are ready to use the topping, it should be brought to room temperature or, in some cases, gently heated; then all you need to do is mindlessly cook a pot of noodles. These uncooked toppings are just the thing when you are particularly rushed, or when you can't stand the heat in the summer and just need to get out of the kitchen.

The pestos, salsas, and fresh sauce recipes in this chapter are flavorful enough to stand on their own when tossed with noodles. (Each recipe for salsa, pesto, or uncooked sauce is enough for 16 ounces of dried pasta, cooked.) In their simplicity, the dishes also make excellent side-dish accompaniments. To use them as main courses, I often add steamed, sautéed, or uncooked vegetables and strips of cooked chicken or seafood to add substance. With each recipe I have provided serving suggestions, but use your imagination and let your creativity take over. You'll find pestos can be a great way to dress odds and ends of leftover pasta with odds and ends of vegetables. Because their uses are so varied, the nutritional analysis of the recipes in this chapter are for typical serving amounts: 1 tablespoon of pesto, $1/2$ cup of salsa, and 2 tablespoons of the fresh sauces.

Here are some hints:

- Wash fresh herbs and dry them thoroughly before making pesto.

- Before food processors, cooks used a mortar and pestle to pound ingredients into a tasty pesto. A blender can do the job, but I consider a food processor to be essential gear for making pesto.

- As the pesto ingredients are being combined in your food processor, use a rubber spatula to scrape down the sides occasionally to ensure the pesto will have an even consistency.

- Don't overprocess. Nuts should remain slightly chunky, not puréed to a peanut-butter consistency. Bits of fresh herbs will be visible.

- Covered and refrigerated, pestos will keep for up to 2 days; some can be frozen. After setting, some may thicken and not be fluid enough to coat the pasta. Add some chicken broth (page 188), vegetable broth, or even a little of the pasta cooking water to lighten the sauce before tossing it with the noodles.

- Salsas must be used fresh—never freeze them.

- Bring pestos and salsas to room temperature before tossing with hot, freshly cooked noodles; uncooked sauces, such as the Ricotta-Walnut Sauce (page 124) should be gently heated. If necessary, toss the sauce and noodles together in a large pot over medium heat just until the mixture is heated through.

- Always toss pesto with hot noodles, then chill the mixture if you plan to serve the dish cold.

- These pestos and salsas are great to have on hand in the refrigerator, where they will keep for up to 2 days. Scoop out a few tablespoons of the mixture and toss with noodles to make a quick single serving or even a snack.

- Adjust the seasonings for pestos, salsas, and uncooked sauces after tossing them with the noodles; on their own, the flavors may seem too strong or salty.

- In addition to tossing the pestos with plain noodles, some can contribute to other pasta recipes, such as adding Roasted Red Pepper-Walnut Pesto (page 111) to Mostaccioli with a Trio of Sweet Peppers (page 3) or Basil Pesto (page 100) to Menton Soup (page 200). Pestos can also embellish soups or salad dressings; some can serve as sandwich spreads or as appetizer spreads for crackers.

basil
pesto

Makes ¹/₂ cup—enough for 16 ounces pasta—6 servings

If you're a basil lover—and who isn't?—you'll bless the day you loaded up your freezer with plenty of this reduced-fat Basil Pesto! In the summer I grow my own basil and find this is an ideal way to preserve it at the end of the season before the tender leaves freeze. In addition to any recipes that call for Basil Pesto, you can simply toss this pesto with cooked pasta, such as rainbow rotini and with chunks of plum tomatoes. For variety, toss the pesto with cooked rice to use as an accompaniment for chicken.

1¹/₂ cups loosely packed fresh basil leaves (fresh is essential)

¹/₄ cup pine nuts, preferably toasted (see Tips)

2 tablespoons extra-virgin olive oil

2 teaspoons minced garlic

¹/₄ teaspoon pepper, or to taste

Dash of salt, or to taste

GARNISH (OPTIONAL)   freshly ground black pepper, freshly grated Parmesan cheese

1. Put all of the ingredients into a food processor; process, using a rubber spatula to scrape down the sides occasionally, until the mixture is a coarse purée.

2. Toss with hot, freshly cooked pasta. Adjust the seasonings to taste.

PER TABLESPOON: Cal 63/Prot .7g/Carb 1.9g/Fat 6.4g/Chol 0mg/Sod 23mg

ADVANCE PREPARATION   Spoon the mixture into a jar and pour a thin film of oil on top to prevent discoloration. Cover and refrigerate for up to 2 days. Bring to room temperature before tossing with hot, freshly cooked pasta. To freeze, spoon the mixture, in 2-tablespoon quantities,

into foil-lined custard cups or muffin tins. Cover tightly with foil and freeze. Once frozen, remove the foil-wrapped packets and place them in a freezer bag for up to 2 months. To use, allow to thaw in the refrigerator overnight, or remove from the foil and thaw quickly in the microwave. Bring to room temperature before tossing with hot, freshly cooked pasta.

TIPS

- Pine nuts (also called pignoli nuts, pignolia, or piñons) are the seeds from the cone of certain pine trees. Their natural oil turns rancid very quickly, so they should be refrigerated for no more than 1 month or frozen for up to 3 months.

- The sweet, mild flavor of pine nuts is enhanced by toasting: Put the pine nuts in a small dry skillet over medium heat; stir constantly and watch carefully for 4 to 5 minutes or until the nuts are lightly browned. Or pine nuts can be toasted in the oven: Spread a single layer of nuts on an ungreased baking sheet; bake at 375°F for 4 to 5 minutes, stirring frequently. Immediately remove the nuts from the pan as soon as they are browned. I usually toast 1 cup at a time and then freeze the nuts until I need them. Toasted pine nuts make a delicious garnish for pasta dishes, soups, and salads.

spinach-parsley pesto

Makes 1 cup—enough for 16 ounces pasta—6 servings

This makes a delicious alternative to Basil Pesto when fresh basil is unavailable. By combining spinach with basil, the flavor is milder. For a colorful mix, toss the Spinach-Parsley Pesto with penne and steamed carrot strips, which also add a touch of sweetness. Garnish each serving with freshly grated Parmesan cheese.

2 cups coarsely chopped stemmed spinach leaves (see Tip)

1 cup fresh flat-leaf parsley sprigs

1/4 cup toasted pine nuts

2 tablespoons extra-virgin olive oil

1 teaspoon minced garlic

1/2 teaspoon pepper, or to taste

1/8 teaspoon salt, or to taste

GARNISH (OPTIONAL) freshly ground black pepper, freshly grated Parmesan cheese

1. Put all of the ingredients into a food processor; process until the mixture is a slightly chunky purée.

2. Toss with hot, freshly cooked pasta. Adjust the seasonings to taste.

PER TABLESPOON: Cal 33/Prot .6g/Carb 1.2g/Fat 3.2g/Chol 0mg/Sod 25mg

ADVANCE PREPARATION Covered and refrigerated, this pesto will keep for up to 2 days. Bring to room temperature before tossing with hot, freshly cooked pasta.

TIP

When buying fresh spinach, look for springy, bright leaves and short stems. In general, the smaller the spinach leaves, the more tender and more delicately flavored the vegetable will be. Salad spinach, sold in most supermarkets, is tender, young, spinach leaves that have been prewashed before packaging. If the leaves seem wilted, wrap them in moist paper towels and refrigerate to revive.

parsley-pecan
pesto

Makes 1 cup—enough for 16 ounces pasta—6 servings

This nutty-tasting pesto is adapted from a recipe in my cookbook, The 15-Minute Single Gourmet. *When there is no time to shop and very little time to cook, I toss this simple sauce, made from staples, with rainbow rotini and chunks of plum tomatoes.*

1 cup fresh flat-leaf parsley sprigs, loosely packed

1/2 cup coarsely chopped pecans, preferably toasted (see Tips)

1/4 cup freshly grated Parmesan cheese

2 tablespoons minced fresh basil (or 1 teaspoon dried basil)

2 tablespoons extra-virgin olive oil

1 tablespoon fresh lemon juice

2 teaspoons minced garlic

1 teaspoon pepper, or to taste

Dash of salt, or to taste

GARNISH (OPTIONAL)   freshly ground black pepper, freshly grated Parmesan cheese, sprigs of fresh flat-leaf parsley

1. Put all of the ingredients into a food processor; process until the mixture is a slightly chunky purée.

2. Toss with hot, freshly cooked pasta. Adjust the seasonings to taste.

PER TABLESPOON: Cal 48/Prot 1.1/Carb 1.4g/Fat 4.5g/Chol 1mg/Sod 39mg

ADVANCE PREPARATION   Covered and refrigerated, this pesto will keep for up to 2 days. Bring to room temperature before tossing with hot, freshly cooked pasta.

TIPS

- Because of their high fat content, nuts quickly become rancid at room temperature. Shelled nuts can be refrigerated in an airtight container for up to 4 months or frozen for up to 6 months. To freshen their flavor, spread the nuts on a baking sheet and heat in a 150°F oven for a few minutes.

- Toasting enhances the flavor of most nuts. To toast nuts on the stovetop, put them into a dry skillet over medium-high heat. Watch closely as you stir or toss them for about 4 to 5 minutes or until they are golden brown. If you prefer, nuts can be toasted on a baking sheet or pie plate in a 375°F oven for about 5 to 10 minutes, stirring frequently. Prevent burning by removing the nuts from the skillet or baking pan as soon as they are toasted.

roasted sweet red pepper **pesto**

Makes 1 cup—enough for 16 ounces pasta—6 servings

For speedy preparation, use commercially prepared roasted red bell peppers available in jars in most supermarkets. When time permits, I prefer using 2 home-roasted peppers (see Tip). This lively pesto (especially so with an added dash of red pepper flakes) is compatible with nearly any pasta.

TIP

To roast a bell pepper: Position the oven broiler rack about 3 inches from the heating element and preheat the broiler. Cut the bell pepper in half lengthwise; discard the seeds, membranes, and stem. Place the pepper halves, skin sides up, on a foil-lined baking sheet; flatten each with the palm of your hand (or cut each pepper half into 2 length-wise strips.) Lightly brushing the skins with olive oil will add additional flavor. Broil for about 8 to 10 minutes or until the peppers are fork tender and the skins are charred and blistered. While they are still hot, transfer the pepper halves to a zip-top plastic bag and seal; set aside for 10 to 15 minutes. (The steam will loosen the skins.) Remove from the bag; peel and discard the skins.

1 (12-ounce) jar roasted red bell peppers, drained (see (See Tip)

2 tablespoons extra-virgin olive oil

2 tablespoons red wine vinegar

2 teaspoons minced garlic

1/4 teaspoon pepper, or to taste

Dash of salt, or to taste

Pinch of red pepper flakes, or to taste

2 tablespoons capers, drained and rinsed

GARNISH (OPTIONAL)   freshly ground black pepper, freshly grated Parmesan cheese or chèvre cheese

1. Put all of the ingredients, except the capers, into a food processor; process until the mixture is thick and smooth. Stir in the capers.

2. Toss with hot, freshly cooked pasta. Adjust the seasonings to taste.

PER TABLESPOON: Cal 23/Prot .1g/Carb 1.8g/Fat 1.7g/Chol 0mg/Sod 64mg

ADVANCE PREPARATION   Covered and refrigerated, this pesto will keep for 2 days. Bring to room temperature before tossing with hot, freshly cooked pasta.

black **olive-tomato** pesto

Makes 1 cup—enough for 16 ounces pasta—6 servings

For a quick, winning weeknight dinner, toss this unusual pesto with spaghetti or linguine; add garbanzos or other beans, strips of sautéed or grilled chicken, thawed baby shrimp, or a (6-ounce) can of water-packed solid white albacore tuna (drained and flaked).

1 (4-ounce) can chopped ripe black olives, drained

1/4 cup fat-free low-sodium chicken broth

1/4 cup tomato paste (see Tip)

2 tablespoons extra-virgin olive oil (see Tip)

2 tablespoons red wine vinegar

1 tablespoon minced fresh oregano (or 1 teaspoon dried oregano)

2 teaspoons minced garlic

1/2 teaspoon pepper, or to taste

1/4 teaspoon salt, or to taste

GARNISH (OPTIONAL)   freshly ground black pepper, freshly grated Parmesan cheese or crumbled feta cheese

1. Put all of the ingredients into a food processor; process until the mixture is nearly smooth.

2. Toss with hot, freshly cooked pasta. Adjust the seasonings to taste.

PER TABLESPOON: Cal 32/Prot .3g/Carb 1.7g/Fat 3g/ Chol 0mg/Sod 103mg

ADVANCE PREPARATION   Covered and refrigerated, this pesto will keep for up to 2 days or freeze for up to 2 months. Allow to thaw in the refrigerator overnight and bring to room temperature before tossing with hot, freshly cooked pasta.

> ## TIPS
>
> - Tomato paste is available in tubes, ideal for recipes needing less than a 6-ounce can. Refrigerate after opening.
>
> - Olive oil is used when its fruity flavor and distinctive aroma is compatible with the other ingredients; "extra-virgin," the most full-bodied and flavorful olive oil, is the best choice in uncooked recipes like pestos, salsas, or salad dressings (its flavor dissipates somewhat when heated). Recipes with Asian flavors provided by soy sauce, sesame oil, and ginger call for a neutral cooking oil. In these recipes, use canola or safflower oil.

creamy **four-herb pesto**

Makes $^3/_4$ cup—enough for 16 ounces pasta—6 servings

In addition to spring flowers, I always plant pots of herbs on the deck near my kitchen. The mid-summer results of my efforts inspired this aromatic blend of flavors. Tossed with a short cut pasta, such as ziti, chunky pieces of grilled chicken breast, steamed fresh summer vegetables, and chunks of garden-fresh tomatoes, the feast is complete. Just add a green salad and warm crusty bread.

$^1/_2$ cup chèvre cheese

$^1/_2$ cup sprigs of fresh flat-leaf parsley

$^1/_2$ cup fresh basil leaves

$^1/_4$ cup fat-free low-sodium chicken broth

$^1/_4$ cup coarsely chopped shallots

1 tablespoon extra-virgin olive oil

1 tablespoon fresh thyme leaves (see Tip)

2 teaspoons minced garlic

1 teaspoon coarsely chopped fresh
   rosemary leaves

$^1/_2$ teaspoon pepper, or to taste

Dash of salt, or to taste

TIP

To use fresh thyme leaves, hold a sprig between your thumb and forefinger and gently strip the leaves from the stem. Use the leaves whole or minced, or crush them with a mortar and pestle. Thyme, with its light-lemon aroma, is pungent whether it is fresh or dried, so use it in moderate amounts.

GARNISH (OPTIONAL) sprigs of fresh herbs, plum tomato slices, freshly grated Romano cheese

1. Put all of the ingredients into a food processor. Process until the consistency is nearly smooth.

2. Toss with hot, freshly cooked pasta. Adjust the seasonings to taste.

PER TABLESPOON: Cal 28/Prot .9g/Carb 1.1g/Fat 2.1g/Chol 5mg/Sod 62mg

ADVANCE PREPARATION   Covered and refrigerated, this will keep for up to 2 days. Bring to room temperature before tossing with hot, freshly cooked pasta.

Sun-Dried Tomato Pesto with fusilli
(page 108)

sun-dried
tomato
pesto

Makes 1 cup—enough for 16 ounces pasta—6 servings

Because it takes 17 pounds of fresh tomatoes to make 1 pound of dried tomatoes, this pesto is intensely flavored. For simple elegance, toss it with fusilli and sliced cremini or portobello mushrooms that have been lightly sautéed in olive oil. And, personally, I think the perfect finishing touch is a garnish of creamy chèvre cheese, added while the pasta is hot so that it melts into the dish.

1 (6-ounce) jar oil-packed minced sun-dried tomatoes ($3/4$ cup); drain and reserve oil (see Tips)

1 tablespoon olive oil (or use reserved oil from the sun-dried tomatoes)

$1/4$ cup coarsely chopped fresh flat-leaf parsley

2 tablespoons fresh lemon juice

1 teaspoon minced garlic

$1/4$ teaspoon pepper, or to taste

$1/8$ teaspoon red pepper flakes, or to taste

Dash of salt, or to taste

GARNISH (OPTIONAL)   freshly ground black pepper, toasted pine nuts, freshly grated Parmesan cheese or chèvre cheese

1. Stir together all of the ingredients in a medium bowl.

2. Toss with hot, freshly cooked pasta. Adjust the seasonings to taste.

PER TABLESPOON: Cal 38/Prot 1.3g/Carb 7.5g/Fat .9g/Chol 0mg/Sod 22mg

ADVANCE PREPARATION   Covered and refrigerated, this pesto will keep for up to 2 days. Bring to room temperature before tossing with hot, freshly cooked pasta.

TIPS

- Because of their superior flavor and ease of use, I prefer to purchase jars of sun-dried tomatoes that have been rehydrated and packed in olive oil; they must be refrigerated after opening. Drain off the excess oil before using. (The oil can be saved, refrigerated, and used in recipes calling for olive oil, especially recipes with tomatoes as an ingredient.)

- Dried tomatoes will keep in an airtight container for several months and must be rehydrated before using in many recipes. Cover them with boiling water and allow to soak for about 10 to 15 minutes, depending on how soft you want them; then drain off the water. Use immediately or marinate in olive oil (be sure to refrigerate) for use later. In both the dried and oil-packed forms, the tomatoes are packaged whole, halved, julienned, or already chopped or minced; to chop them yourself, the easiest method is to use kitchen shears.

vegetable pesto

Makes 2 cups—enough for 16 ounces pasta—8 servings

Even when it is made in advance, this pesto has a very clean, fresh taste that is at its best when tossed with fresh angel hair pasta and topped with grilled or sautéed butterflied shrimp and crumbled feta cheese.

2 cups plum tomatoes in $^1/_2$-inch cubes

2 ribs celery with leaves, coarsely chopped (about $^1/_2$ cup)

$^1/_2$ cup fresh flat-leaf parsley sprigs

$^1/_4$ cup olive oil–packed chopped sun-dried tomatoes; drain and reserve oil

2 tablespoons extra-virgin olive oil (or use reserved oil from the sun-dried tomatoes)

2 tablespoons red wine vinegar

2 teaspoons minced garlic

$^1/_2$ teaspoon sugar

$^1/_2$ teaspoon pepper, or to taste (see Tip)

$^1/_4$ teaspoon salt, or to taste

Pinch of red pepper flakes, or to taste

TIP

Freshly ground or cracked whole dried peppercorns are more flavorful than preground pepper because, once cracked, the peppercorn immediately releases much of its oil as aroma and flavor. The best pepper grinders have settings for both coarse and fine grinds. To measure, grind the pepper onto a sheet of waxed paper and pour into a measuring spoon. Store whole peppercorns in a cool, dark place for up to 1 year.

GARNISH (OPTIONAL)   freshly ground black pepper, crumbled feta cheese

1. Put all of the ingredients into a food processor; process until the mixture is creamy and nearly smooth.

2. Toss with hot, freshly cooked pasta. Adjust the seasonings to taste.

PER TABLESPOON: Cal 32/Prot .6g/Carb 2.6g/Fat 2.3g/ Chol 0mg/Sod 43mg

ADVANCE PREPARATION   Covered and refrigerated, this pesto will keep for up to 2 days. Bring to room temperature before tossing with hot, freshly cooked pasta.

roasted red pepper– walnut pesto

Makes 1¹/₄ cups—enough for 16 ounces pasta—6 servings

This colorful pesto has a robust flavor. Toss it with farfalle (bow ties) and add nothing but a garnish of toasted chopped walnuts. Serve the dish solo as an entrée or as a winsome accompaniment to grilled chicken breasts. If you have extra pesto, it can be added to other pasta recipes, such as Mostaccioli with a Trio of Sweet Peppers (page 3).

1 (12-ounce) jar roasted red bell peppers, drained

¹/₂ cup coarsely chopped walnuts (see Tip), preferably toasted

2 tablespoons roasted walnut oil

2 tablespoons red wine vinegar

1 teaspoon minced garlic

¹/₂ teaspoon pepper, or to taste

¹/₄ teaspoon salt, or to taste

GARNISH (OPTIONAL)   freshly ground black pepper, freshly grated Parmesan cheese, toasted chopped walnuts, sprigs of fresh flat-leaf parsley

1. Put all of the ingredients into a food processor; process until the peppers are puréed and the walnuts remain slightly chunky.

2. Toss with hot, freshly cooked pasta. Adjust the seasonings to taste.

PER TABLESPOON: Cal 34/Prot .9g/Carb 1.1g/Fat 3.1g/Chol 0mg/Sod 27mg

Variation:

• Substitute 2 freshly roasted red bell peppers for the jar of bell peppers.

ADVANCE PREPARATION   Covered and refrigerated, this pesto will keep for up to 2 days. Bring to room temperature before tossing with hot, freshly cooked pasta.

> ### TIP
>
> There are two kinds of walnuts. Black walnuts are stronger in flavor than English (or Persian) walnuts. (Either can be used in this recipe.) Shelled walnuts can be tightly covered and refrigerated for up to 6 months or frozen for up to 1 year.

cilantro-citrus
pesto

Makes ¹/₂ cup—enough for 8 ounces pasta—4 servings

*Blending the distinctive flavors of cilantro and citrus juices is a marriage
made in heaven. Toss this with thin Chinese wheat-flour noodles and top with
sautéed or grilled shrimp.*

1 cup sprigs of fresh cilantro, tender stems included (see Tip)

¹/₄ cup minced shallots

2 tablespoons roasted peanut oil (see Tip)

2 tablespoons fresh lime juice

2 tablespoons fresh orange juice

2 teaspoons minced fresh ginger

1 teaspoon chili paste with garlic, or to taste

Dash of pepper, or to taste

Dash of salt, or to taste

GARNISH (OPTIONAL)   finely chopped unsalted dry-roasted peanuts, sprigs
of fresh cilantro

1. Put all of the ingredients into a food processor; process until the
    mixture is nearly smooth.

2. Toss with hot, freshly cooked noodles. Adjust the seasonings to taste.

PER TABLESPOON: Cal 38/Prot .3g/Carb 2g/Fat 3.4g/Chol 0mg/Sod 27mg

TIPS

- Cilantro, often sold as "fresh coriander" or
  "Chinese parsley," is a cornerstone of
  Vietnamese, Thai, Asian, Indian, and
  Mexican cuisines. Choose leaves with a
  bright, even color and no sign of wilting.
  They are often used uncooked. If adding to
  a cooked recipe, do so near the end of the
  cooking period to retain full flavor. The
  dried leaves lack the distinctive flavor of
  fresh cilantro and are an unacceptable
  substitution. Ground coriander, an ingredient in most curry powders, is made from
  the ground seeds of the plant and serves a
  different purpose in cooking from that of
  coriander leaves.

- Roasted peanut oil is made from peanuts
  that are dry-roasted prior to pressing; the
  aroma and flavor are far superior to that of
  other peanut oils. Roasted peanut oil is
  available in some supermarkets and gourmet shops.

Hazelnut and Sage Pesto with ravioli
(page 114)

hazlenut and sage pesto

Makes ³/₄ cup—enough for 8 ounces ravioli—4 servings

My guests have savored this distinctive pesto tossed with pumpkin-filled ravioli (available in the fall at some Italian specialty shops) and garnished with a sprinkling of brilliant red pomegranate seeds (see Tip). Or simply combine the pesto with cheese-filled ravioli or tortellini and garnish with freshly grated Parmesan cheese.

¹/₃ cup hazelnuts (see Tip), preferably toasted

2 tablespoons coarsely chopped walnuts, preferably toasted

2 tablespoons roasted walnut oil

1 tablespoon crushed dried sage leaves (or 1 teaspoon rubbed sage)

1 teaspoon minced garlic

¹/₄ teaspoon pepper, or to taste

¹/₂ cup freshly grated Parmesan cheese

GARNISH (OPTIONAL)   freshly ground black pepper

1. Put all of the ingredients, except the Parmesan cheese, into a food processor. Process until the mixture is a slightly chunky purée. Stir in the Parmesan cheese.

2. Toss with hot, freshly cooked pasta. Adjust the seasoning to taste.

PER TABLESPOON: Cal 68/Prot 2.5g/Carb 1g/Fat 6.2g/Chol 3mg/Sod 78mg

ADVANCE PREPARATION   Covered and refrigerated, this pesto will keep for up to 2 days. Bring to room temperature before tossing with hot, freshly cooked pasta.

TIPS

- A pomegranate is a fruit the size of a large orange, ranging in color from red to pink-blushed yellow. Inside are hundreds of tiny, edible seeds surrounded by a bright red pulp that has a sweet-tart flavor; cut the fruit in half to pry out the seeds. In the United States, pomegranates are available in October and November. Refrigerated, they will keep for up to 2 months.

- Hazelnuts, or filberts, have a bitter brown skin that should be removed: Spread them in a single layer on an ungreased baking sheet and bake at 350°F for 10 to 15 minutes, or until the skins begin to flake. Pour about $1/4$ cup of the nuts into a dish towel, fold over the sides of the towel, and rub vigorously until most of the skin on each nut is removed. The toasting also enhances the flavor of the nuts. Like other nuts, store hazelnuts in the refrigerator for up to 4 months or in the freezer for up to 6 months; they will become rancid at room temperature in 2 months.

lemony **tomato** salsa

Makes 3 cups—enough for 16 ounces pasta—6 servings

Some cooks peel, seed, or salt tomatoes to enhance the flavor and texture of tomato sauces. I eliminate those steps when using juicy summer tomatoes or top-quality hydroponic tomatoes in the winter. I like to toss this chunky salsa with penne and allow the refreshing mixture to come to room temperature before serving it solo as a pasta salad or as a colorful accompaniment to grilled chicken.

3 tablespoons fresh lemon juice (see Tips)

2 tablespoons extra-virgin olive oil

2 tablespoons balsamic vinegar

1 teaspoon minced garlic

$1/2$ teaspoon pepper, or to taste

$1/4$ teaspoon red pepper flakes, or to taste

$1/8$ teaspoon salt, or to taste

$1/8$ teaspoon sugar

3 large beefsteak tomatoes (at room temperature), cut into $1/2$-inch cubes

2 tablespoons coarsely chopped fresh basil

1 tablespoon coarsely chopped fresh flat-leaf parsley

GARNISH (OPTIONAL)   freshly ground black pepper, freshly grated Parmesan cheese, sprigs of fresh basil or fresh flat-leaf parsley

1. Whisk together the lemon juice, oil, vinegar, garlic, black pepper, red pepper flakes, salt, and sugar in a small bowl. Set aside.

2. Gently stir together the tomatoes, basil, and parsley in a medium bowl. Add the lemon juice mixture and toss.

3. If possible, allow the salsa to stand at room temperature for about 30 minutes before tossing with hot, freshly cooked pasta. Adjust the seasonings to taste.

4. Serve warm or allow to cool.

PER ¼ CUP: Cal 29/Prot .3g/Carb 2.3g/Fat 2.4g/Chol 0mg/Sod 26mg

TIPS

- Freshly squeezed citrus juice is always the most flavorful. Frozen pure juice is also acceptable. Avoid the chemical-laden and artificial-tasting reconstituted lemon and lime juices that come in bottles and plastic "lemons" and "limes."

- To squeeze more juice from citrus fruits, first bring them to room temperature; or microwave chilled fruit (pierce the fruit with a fork or knife first) for 30 seconds on high. Then roll the fruit around on a hard surface for a minute or so, pressing hard with the palm of your hand, to break the inner membranes. If you need only a small amount of juice, save the fruit for future use by making a deep X-shaped incision into the fruit with a paring knife. Squeeze out the juice you need; then store the fruit in a sealed plastic bag in the refrigerator.

salsa
provençal

Makes 4 cups—enough for 8 ounces pasta—6 servings

Provençal refers to the style of Provence, a region in southeastern France, where the ingredients in this salsa are plentiful. All of them are available in jars on supermarket shelves, and they can be stored in your pantry, ready to be tossed together on a moment's notice. I think the giant fava beans are especially appealing when tossed with gnocchi because both ingredients have a unique and bulbous shape; but any short-cut chunky pasta will do. The mixture is delicious served warm; but since this makes a plentiful amount, I enjoy having it on hand to serve with pasta (at room temperature) for lunch.

1 (19-ounce) can fava beans, drained and rinsed (see Tip)

1 (7-ounce) jar roasted red bell peppers, drained and coarsely chopped

1/4 cup sliced Kalamata olives (about 10 pitted olives)

1 (6-ounce) jar marinated quartered artichoke hearts, drained

2 tablespoons extra-virgin olive oil

2 tablespoons red wine vinegar

2 tablespoons minced fresh basil (or 1 teaspoon dried basil)

1 tablespoon capers, drained and rinsed

1 teaspoon minced garlic, or to taste

1/2 teaspoon pepper, or to taste

1/4 teaspoon salt, or to taste

1/8 teaspoon red pepper flakes, or to taste

GARNISH (OPTIONAL)   freshly ground black pepper, freshly grated Parmesan cheese or crumbled feta cheese

1. Stir together all of the ingredients in a medium bowl.

2. Toss with hot, freshly cooked pasta. Adjust the seasonings to taste.

PER ¼ CUP: Cal 63/Prot 1.9g/Carb 7.8g/Fat 2.8g/Chol 0mg/Sod 237mg

Variations:

- Substitute other beans, such as cannellini beans, for the fava beans.

- Substitute 2 freshly roasted red bell peppers for the jar of bell peppers.

ADVANCE PREPARATION   Covered and refrigerated, this salsa will keep for up to 2 days if made with dried basil. If using fresh basil, add it just before tossing the salsa with pasta. The completed dish will keep in a covered container in the refrigerator for up to 2 days.

> ### TIP
>
> Fava beans are dark-skinned beans that look like very large lima beans. They are rarely found fresh but can be purchased dried or in cans in many supermarkets. Fava beans are popular in Mediterranean and Middle Eastern dishes.

mediterranean
tomato-basil
salsa

Makes 3 cups—enough for 16 ounces pasta—6 servings

Try this easy recipe for a dinner party.

Combine the salsa ingredients early in the day. Minutes before you seat your guests, toss a green salad, heat a loaf of bread, and toss the salsa with hot, freshly cooked penne rigate. Or, if you prefer, combine the salsa with penne several hours ahead and serve the dish at room temperature. Your guests will never need to know you spent only 15 minutes making the meal.

1 large tomato, cut into $1/2$-inch cubes (about 1 cup)

1 (6-ounce) jar marinated artichoke hearts, drained and coarsely chopped (see Tip)

$1/2$ cup oil-packed diced sun-dried tomatoes, drained

2 tablespoons capers, drained and rinsed

1 tablespoon extra-virgin olive oil

1 tablespoon fresh lemon juice

1 teaspoon minced garlic

$1/2$ teaspoon pepper, or to taste

$1/4$ teaspoon salt, or to taste

$1/2$ cup coarsely chopped fresh basil

$1/4$ cup freshly grated Parmesan cheese

GARNISH (OPTIONAL)   freshly ground black pepper, crumbled feta cheese, lemon wedges, sprigs of fresh basil

1. Stir together all of the ingredients, except the basil and Parmesan cheese, in a medium bowl. Cover and let stand at room temperature for about 30 minutes. (Or cover and refrigerate for up to 1 day.)

2. If refrigerated, bring to room temperature. Add the basil and Parmesan cheese. Toss with hot, freshly cooked pasta. Adjust the seasonings to taste.

PER ¼ CUP: Cal 112/Prot 5.2g/Carb 17.8g/Fat 3.8g/Chol 3mg/Sod 254mg

ADVANCE PREPARATION   Covered and refrigerated, this salsa will keep for up to 1 day. The completed dish will keep in the refrigerator for up to 1 additional day. Bring to room temperature before tossing with hot, freshly cooked pasta.

> ## TIP
>
> Artichoke hearts are the tender portions remaining after the tough leaves have been removed from whole artichokes. Artichoke hearts are available marinated in jars or unmarinated in cans.

greek **tomato-olive** salsa

Makes 2 cups—enough for 16 ounces pasta—6 servings

Compared with the familiar bland California canned olives, imported olives are so succulent that only a few per serving are necessary to add a vibrant Mediterranean flair. Toss this salsa with spaghetti and serve warm or chilled, garnished with feta cheese to add a flavor complement.

1 (15-ounce) can diced tomatoes, with juice

1/4 cup coarsely chopped red onion

2 tablespoons sliced Kalamata olives (about 5 pitted olives); (see Tip)

1 tablespoon extra-virgin olive oil

1/4 cup coarsely chopped fresh flat-leaf parsley

2 teaspoons minced fresh marjoram (or 1/2 teaspoon dried marjoram)

2 teaspoons minced fresh thyme (or 1/2 teaspoon dried thyme)

1 teaspoon minced garlic, or to taste

1/2 teaspoon pepper, or to taste

> ## TIP
>
> Kalamata olives are eggplant-colored, almond-shaped Greek olives, ranging in length from about 1/2 to 1 inch. The rich and fruity-flavored olives are packed in olive oil, brine, or wine vinegar. The olives are often slit to allow the marinade in which they're soaked to be absorbed into the flesh.

GARNISH (OPTIONAL) freshly ground black pepper, crumbled feta cheese

1. Stir together all of the ingredients in a medium bowl.

2. Allow the mixture to stand at room temperature for about 30 minutes before tossing with hot, freshly cooked pasta. Adjust the seasonings to taste.

PER 1/4 CUP: Cal 40/Prot .7g/Carb 3.8g/Fat 2.8g/Chol 0mg/Sod 186mg

ADVANCE PREPARATION Covered and refrigerated, this pesto will keep for up to 2 days. Bring to room temperature before tossing with hot, freshly cooked pasta.

Variation:

• Add red pepper flakes, to taste, for a hotter flavor.

fresh
basil, tomato,
and **mozzarella** toss

Makes 3 cups—enough for 16 ounces pasta—6 servings

This simple mixture requires top-quality fresh ingredients. Pour it over hot, freshly cooked linguine and toss gently. I prefer to serve this dish immediately, but I also enjoy the delicious leftovers right out of the refrigerator for lunch the next day.

1 large ripe beefsteak tomato (at room temperature), cut into 1/2-inch cubes (see Tips)

1/4 pound fresh mozzarella cheese, cut into 1/2-inch cubes (see Tip)

1/2 cup fresh basil chiffonade

1/4 cup extra-virgin olive oil

2 teaspoons minced garlic

1/2 teaspoon pepper, or to taste

1/4 teaspoon salt, or to taste

Pinch of red pepper flakes, or to taste

GARNISH (OPTIONAL)   freshly ground black pepper, freshly grated Parmesan cheese

1. Mix the ingredients in a medium bowl.

2. If possible, let stand at room temperature for 30 minutes to 1 hour to allow the flavors to blend before tossing with hot, freshly cooked pasta. Adjust the seasonings to taste.

PER 1/4 CUP: Cal 68/Prot 2.5g/Carb 1.2g/Fat 6.1g/Chol 5mg/Sod 90mg

---

TIPS

- Because cool temperatures reduce the flavor of tomatoes and can make their texture mealy, do not store them in the refrigerator. On the counter at room temperature, tomatoes will continue to get redder, softer, juicier, and tastier; once they are fully ripened, use within 2 days.

- To prevent tearing and bruising, use a knife with a serrated stainless-steel blade for slicing and cutting tomatoes.

- Fresh, "Italian style," mozzarella cheese is usually packaged in whey or water. Generally, it is made from whole milk and has a softer texture and a sweeter, milder flavor than regular packaged mozzarella. The fresh form is found in Italian markets, cheese shops, and in some supermarkets.

chapter 2 Pestos, Salsas, and Fresh Sauces

123

ricotta-walnut
sauce

Makes 1 cup—enough for 16 ounces pasta—6 servings

When tossing this creamy, nutty-flavored sauce with mafalda (mini lasagna), I add peas, broccoli florets, or cut green beans, and a garnish of cherry tomatoes for a burst of color.

1/2 cup nonfat ricotta cheese

1/2 cup nonfat plain yogurt

1/2 cup coarsely chopped walnuts, preferably toasted

1 tablespoon butter, softened

1 teaspoon minced garlic or roasted garlic (see Tips)

3/4 teaspoon pepper, or to taste

Dash of salt, or to taste

1/4 cup freshly grated Parmesan cheese

1/2 cup coarsely chopped fresh flat-leaf parsley

1/4 cup minced fresh basil (or 1 teaspoon dried basil)

GARNISH (OPTIONAL)   freshly ground black pepper, cherry tomatoes, sprigs of flat-leaf parsley

1. Put all of the ingredients, except the Parmesan cheese, parsley, and basil, into a food processor; process until the mixture is a slightly chunky purée. Transfer to a small saucepan. Stir over low heat just until warm. (Do not let the sauce come to a boil.)

2. Toss with hot, freshly cooked pasta in a large pot over low heat. Remove from the heat; toss in the Parmesan cheese, parsley, and basil. Adjust the seasonings to taste.

PER 2 TABLESPOONS: Cal 94/Prot 5.4g/Carb 4g/Fat 6.8g/Chol 9mg/Sod 117mg

ADVANCE PREPARATION   Cover and refrigerate the ricotta cheese mixture (without the Parmesan cheese, parsley, and basil) for up to 2 days. To use, warm, stirring constantly, over low heat (do not let the mixture come to a boil). If the mixture has thickened, thin by stirring in milk, chicken broth, vegetable stock, or water. Toss the sauce with hot, freshly cooked pasta and add the remaining ingredients.

TIPS

- Store garlic heads in a cool, dark, well-ventilated place or seal in a plastic bag and refrigerate. Unbroken bulbs will keep for up to 2 months; individual cloves will keep for up to 10 days. Sprouted garlic cloves are fine to use but less flavorful.

- Marinated minced garlic is an acceptable alternative to fresh garlic. It is sold in jars in the produce department of most supermarkets. Always use a clean spoon when measuring it from the jar and refrigerate for up to 2 months after opening to avoid bacteria growth. (For reasons of food safety, it is not recommended to mince your own garlic and store it in olive oil.) Avoid using dried garlic, which is bitter and will not provide the distinctive garlic flavor and aroma.

- Garlic develops a bitter taste if permitted to brown, so add it near the end of the cooking period unless there is an abundance of moisture in the pan.

- Roasted garlic can be used in most recipes calling for garlic; and alone, roasted garlic makes a delicious spread for crusty bread-a great pasta accompaniment. First, prepare the bulb by gently removing the loose, excess papery skin; leave the cloves intact. Trim off the top stem and $1/4$ to $1/2$ inch of the garlic head (exposing the cloves directly to the heat speeds up the roasting process). Brush the outer skin and top of the bulb with olive oil. To roast garlic in the oven: Place the prepared garlic bulb on a baking sheet or pan lined with aluminum foil. Bake for 20 to 25 minutes, or until the cloves feel very soft when pierced with the tip of a knife. To roast garlic in the microwave: Place the prepared garlic bulb on a paper towel; microwave on high for 1 minute. Turn the bulb upside down, then microwave for 1 more minute, or until the cloves feel very soft when pierced with the tip of a knife.

fettucine
almost- **alfredo**

Makes 2 cups—enough for 16 ounces pasta—6 servings

Becoming a nutrition-conscious cook doesn't mean you have to give up favorites like Fettucine Alfredo. This is a light version of the classic—delectable but with a fraction of the fat. I toss this sauce with fettucine and often add strips of sautéed chicken breast. For vegetarian dining, substitute vegetable stock for the chicken broth and toss in sliced mushrooms, chopped red bell pepper, and minced shallots that have been sautéed in olive oil.

$1^1/_2$ cups nonfat ricotta cheese (see Tip)

$^3/_4$ cup fat-free low-sodium chicken broth

$^1/_2$ cup freshly grated Parmesan cheese

2 tablespoons fresh lemon juice

1 tablespoon butter, softened

1 tablespoon minced garlic

$^1/_2$ teaspoon pepper, or to taste

$^1/_8$ teaspoon salt, or to taste

2 tablespoons minced fresh flat-leaf parsley (see Tip)

1 tablespoon minced fresh basil (or 1 teaspoon dried basil)

GARNISH (OPTIONAL)   freshly ground black pepper, freshly grated Parmesan cheese, halved cherry tomatoes, minced fresh parsley or sprigs of fresh basil

1. Put all of the ingredients, except the parsley and basil, into a food processor; process until the mixture is smooth and creamy.

2. Transfer the sauce to a small saucepan. Stir in the parsley and basil. Stir the mixture over low heat, just until warm. (Do not let the sauce come to a boil.)

3. Toss the sauce with hot, freshly cooked pasta in a large pot over low heat. Adjust the seasonings to taste.

PER 2 TABLESPOONS: Cal 39/Prot 3.4g/Carb 2.7g/Fat 1.7g/Chol 8mg/Sod 136mg

ADVANCE PREPARATION   Covered and refrigerated, this sauce will keep for up to 2 days. To use, warm, stirring constantly, over low heat (do not let the mixture come to a boil). If the mixture has thickened, thin by stirring in milk, chicken broth, vegetable stock, or water before tossing with hot, freshly cooked pasta.

> ## TIPS
>
> - Ricotta cheese is made from the whey that remains after the production of such cheeses as provolone and mozzarella. The whey is blended with whole or skim milk; ricotta, therefore, is not a true cheese because it is not made from curd.
>
> - To mince parsley very finely, be sure to dry it well with a paper towel or dish towel after cleaning it under cool running water. Wet or damp parsley will stick together in clumps as you mince it with a knife or in a food processor.

chapter 2 *Pestos, Salsas, and Fresh Sauces*

chapter 3

Chilled Noodles

ITALIAN PASTA SALADS, WHILE NOT NECESSARILY

traditional, are now fashionable. On the other hand, Asians

discovered long ago that chilled noodles are irresistibly

appealing when combined with crisp vegetables and a

romatic sesame sauces. Chilled pasta and noodle dishes

have evolved into popular fare for picnics and lunch on the

run. We also serve them year-round on buffet tables for

casual events and as part of the menu for elegant dinner

parties—but we're not talking about macaroni salad swimming in mayonnaise or cold, overcooked spaghetti drowned in bottled Italian dressing.

Today's chilled noodle dishes emphasize freshness and showcase brightly colored fresh vegetables. With dressings made from scratch using top-quality ingredients, the dishes exude robust aromas and vibrant flavors. Some salads are tossed, others more artfully composed. Some are substantial enough to serve as entrées, others make the perfect side dish to accompany grilled or broiled fish, chicken, or meat.

These suggestions will guarantee your success:

- Some pastas and noodles are better choices than others for chilling. Short cut pastas and thin noodles work best. Pasta that is too thick or too large seems chewy when served cold; stuffed pastas are unsatisfactory. Chinese egg noodles hold up well to dressings; cellophane noodles have little flavor on their own, making them an excellent vehicle for spicy dressings.

- Pasta and noodles for chilled dishes should be cooked *al dente* to allow for the softening effect of the dressing.

- Drain the noodles after cooking, then rinse with cold water and drain again. The noodles should remain moist, but too much moisture will dilute the dressing.

- The shape and size of the noodles should match the other ingredients. Strands are best combined with julienned, shredded, or diced vegetables; add more coarsely chopped vegetables to chunky shapes like penne.

- Use top-quality vinegars and oils; in these dishes their flavors will not be altered by the heat of cooking.

- Most dressings are quite strong if tasted alone; dip an ingredient from the salad into the dressing to judge the flavor, then adjust the seasonings.

- Covered and refrigerated, most vinegar-and-oil dressings will keep for up to 1 week, a few days less if the dressing is made with fresh herbs or fresh citrus juice. Creamy dressings will keep for up to 2 days. Dressings can be made in advance and then tossed with freshly cooked pasta and vegetables.

- When a noodle salad stands for a couple of hours or longer, the noodles soak up the dressing and the salad may appear and taste dry. To prevent this from happening, you may want to add just half of the dressing when making the salad. Refrigerate the remainder separately and toss it in just before serving. You can also add some fresh vegetables or herbs to perk up the taste and color.

- Most noodle salads taste best at room temperature or just slightly chilled, not icy cold. Remove them from the refrigerator in time to reach the correct temperature for serving.

- When transporting noodle salads, use caution. If they contain fish, chicken, or dairy products, keep them cold. Vinaigrette-dressed dishes can remain unrefrigerated for hours, but they usually taste better if refrigerated until about 30 minutes before serving.

- Individual noodle salads can be presented with creativity; for example, serve the noodles over a layer of mixed gourmet greens or stuffed into a radicchio leaf "cup."

- Noodle salads or some of their components can be served warm. For example, in the Chicken Stir-Fry Salad with Zesty Orange Dressing (page 164), the warm stir-fry mixture can be served over room-temperature noodles.

chapter 3 *Chilled Noodles*

mediterranean
mostaccioli

Makes 6 servings

My guests rave about this dish. The recipe multiplies well to accommodate large groups, and because it's served at room temperature, you can do all of the preparations in advance and be a guest at your own party. Mound the mixture on your favorite large platter as part of a buffet; add a simple green salad tossed with Italian dressing and a basket of crusty bread. For smaller parties, I sometimes serve the dish warm.

12 ounces mostaccioli (about 4 cups)

1/4 cup red wine vinegar

2 tablespoons olive oil, divided

2 tablespoons capers, drained and rinsed

1 tablespoon fresh thyme leaves (or 1 teaspoon dried thyme)

1 teaspoon pepper, or to taste

Dash of salt, or to taste

4 cups peeled eggplant in 1/2-inch cubes (about 1 pound)

2 cups sliced mushrooms

1 small zucchini, halved lengthwise and cut into 1/4-inch-thick slices

1/4 cup minced shallots

4 plum tomatoes, cut into 1/2-inch cubes (about 2 cups); (see Tip)

1/2 cup crumbled feta cheese (see Tip)

GARNISH (OPTIONAL)   freshly ground black pepper, sprigs of fresh thyme or flat-leaf parsley

1. Bring a large pot of water to a boil over high heat; add salt, then the mostaccioli. When the water returns to a boil, stir occasionally to separate the mostaccioli. Reduce the heat to medium-high and cook for about 12 to 14 minutes, or according to package instructions, until noodles are *al dente*.

2. While the mostaccioli is cooking, combine the vinegar, 1 tablespoon of the oil, capers, fresh thyme (if using), pepper, and salt in a small bowl; set aside.

3. Heat the remaining 1 tablespoon of oil in a large nonstick sauté pan over medium-high heat. Add the eggplant, mushrooms, zucchini, and shallots; cook, stirring occasionally, for about 5 minutes or until the eggplant is tender and lightly browned. Stir in the tomatoes and dried thyme (if using); continue to cook, stirring occasionally, for about 2 more minutes or until the tomatoes are softened. Stir in the vinegar mixture. Remove from the heat, cover, and set aside.

4. When the mostaccioli is done, drain and rinse well in cold water, then drain again.

5. Transfer the mostaccioli to a large bowl. Add the eggplant mixture and toss. Add the feta cheese; toss again. Adjust the seasonings to taste.

PER SERVING: Cal 348/Prot 11.6g/Carb 53.2g/Fat 9.9g/Chol 17mg/Sod 276mg

ADVANCE PREPARATION   This dish can be prepared early the day it is to be served; cover and refrigerate. Bring to room temperature before serving.

TIPS

- Plum tomatoes, often called Italian or Roma tomatoes, have thick, meaty walls, small seeds, little juice, and a rich, sweet flavor. They are the best choice for salads or other recipes that benefit from less juicy tomatoes, which retain their shape after being chopped or sliced.

- Feta cheese is a white Greek cheese with a rich, tangy flavor. Traditionally, it is made with goat's milk or sheep's milk, or a combination; today it is also often made with cow's milk. Fresh feta is crumbly and moist; when mature, it becomes drier and saltier.

pesto chicken salad
with red grapes

Makes 4 servings

This is a great party dish, ideal for serving at room temperature along with crusty bread and crisp wine——followed by a decadent chocolate dessert. When I multiplied it to serve 30 guests at a fall event, the dish received glowing reviews and nearly everyone begged for the recipe.

6 ounces penne rigate (about 2 cups)

12 ounces boneless skinless chicken
  breast halves

Creamy Pesto Dressing

1 cup fresh basil leaves, loosely packed

$1/2$ cup nonfat plain yogurt

2 tablespoons white wine vinegar

2 tablespoons extra-virgin olive oil

$1/2$ teaspoon minced garlic

$1/2$ teaspoon pepper, or to taste

$1/4$ teaspoon salt, or to taste

$1/4$ teaspoon sugar

$1/8$ teaspoon red pepper flakes, or to taste

To Complete the Recipe

1 cup coarsely shredded carrots

1 cup seedless red grapes (see Tip)

2 medium scallions, coarsely chopped

GARNISH (OPTIONAL)   freshly ground black pepper, freshly grated Parmesan cheese, toasted pine nuts, sprigs of fresh basil

1. Bring a medium pot of water to a boil over high heat; add salt, then the penne. When the water returns to a boil, stir occasionally to separate the penne. Reduce the heat to medium-high and cook for about 12 to 14 minutes, or according to package instructions, until noodles are *al dente*.

2. At the same time, pour water into a medium sauté pan, to a level of about $1^1/_2$ inches deep; stir in a dash of salt and bring the water to a boil over high heat. Add the chicken (it should be covered by about $^1/_2$ inch of water). Reduce the heat to medium; cover and simmer for about 8 to 10 minutes or until the chicken is just cooked through.

3. While the penne and chicken are cooking, process the dressing ingredients in a food processor until smooth.

4. When the chicken is done, use a slotted spoon to transfer it to a plate. Cut the chicken into 1-inch squares and allow to cool. (Discard the poaching liquid.)

5. When the penne is done, drain and rinse well in cold water, then drain again.

6. Transfer the penne to a large bowl. Add the chicken, carrots, grapes, and scallions; toss. Add the dressing and toss again. Adjust the seasonings to taste.

PER SERVING: Cal 404/Prot 32.4g/Carb 44.2g/Fat 10.8g/Chol 67mg/Sod 226mg

ADVANCE PREPARATION   The dressing will keep for up to 2 days in a tightly closed container in the refrigerator. The salad can be made early the day it is to be served; cover and refrigerate for up to 1 day. Bring to room temperature before serving.

Variation

• Rather than poaching the chicken breasts, grill them on an outdoor grill or a stovetop grill pan.

TIP

Buy grapes that are plump and firmly attached to their stems. Store them unwashed, in a plastic bag, in the refrigerator for up to 1 week. Since most grapes have been sprayed with insecticide, wash them thoroughly and blot with paper toweling before eating or using.

pasta salad **primavera**
with herbed
tomato sauce

Makes 8 servings

This is the ace up my sleeve. I have often taken this salad along as my contribution to the menu for a lakeside weekend, and I have also multiplied the recipe to serve 150 for a garden party. Everyone raves about its delicious blend of fresh flavors.

16 ounces rotelle or rotini (corkscrew
  pasta)

4 cups broccoli florets

Herbed Tomato Sauce

1 (15-ounce) can tomato sauce

2 tablespoons extra-virgin olive oil

2 tablespoons red wine vinegar

2 teaspoons minced garlic

2 tablespoons minced fresh basil (or
  1 teaspoon dried basil)

2 teaspoons minced fresh oregano (or
  $1/2$ teaspoon dried oregano)

$1/2$ teaspoon sugar

$1/2$ teaspoon pepper, or to taste

$1/4$ teaspoon salt, or to taste

To Complete the Recipe

1 cup frozen baby peas, thawed

1 cup part-skim mozzarella cheese in
  $1/2$-inch cubes

1 red bell pepper, coarsely chopped

4 plum tomatoes, cut into $1/2$-inch cubes

4 medium scallions, coarsely chopped

GARNISH (OPTIONAL) freshly ground black pepper, freshly grated Parmesan cheese, sprigs of fresh basil

1. Bring a large pot of water to a boil over high heat; add salt, then the pasta. When the water returns to a boil, stir once to separate the pasta. Reduce the heat to medium-high and cook for about 8 to 10 minutes, or according to package instructions, until noodles are *al dente*.

2. While the pasta is cooking, put the broccoli into a small microwave-proof dish; add about ¼ cup water. Cover and microwave on high for about 4 minutes or until crisp-tender. (Or cook the broccoli for about 5 minutes in a stovetop steamer.) Drain and rinse well in cold water, then drain again.

3. Stir together the sauce ingredients in a small bowl.

4. When the pasta is done, drain and rinse well in cold water, then drain again.

5. Transfer the pasta to a large bowl. Add the broccoli and the remaining ingredients; toss. Add the sauce and toss again. Adjust the seasonings to taste.

PER SERVING: Cal 345/Prot 15.1g/Carb 54.3g/Fat 7.5g/Chol 10mg/Sod 540mg

ADVANCE PREPARATION   Covered and refrigerated separately, the sauce and the pasta mixture will keep for up to 3 days. Bring to room temperature and add the sauce no more than 1 hour before serving the salad.

Variations

- Substitute other vegetables for the broccoli, peas, or bell pepper (up to 8 cups total). Try steamed carrot slices or cut asparagus.

- Add about 1 pound frozen salad shrimp, thawed; omit the cheese.

> ## TIP
>
> To microwave vegetables, put the vegetables in a microwave-proof dish, add about ¼ cup water, and cover tightly. Microwave all fresh vegetables on the high setting. Cook only until crisp-tender; the cooking continues for about 2 minutes after the dish is removed from the oven.

Creste Di Gallo with Smoked Salmon in Green Peppercorn Sauce

creste di gallo
with salmon
in green peppercorn sauce

Makes 4 servings

Its unique and ornate shape makes creste di gallo, or cock's crest, one of my favorite pastas for salads. Because it is not always available in supermarkets, I always buy a bag or two when I'm at an Italian market. Other more common short cut pastas, such as pipe rigate or farfalle (bow ties) can be substituted.

The pleasant pungency of green peppercorns is a complement to any kind of seafood, from canned albacore tuna to smoked salmon. Serve this at room temperature with crusty breadsticks.

Green Peppercorn Sauce

$1/4$ cup red wine vinegar

2 tablespoons hazelnut oil

1 tablespoon extra-virgin olive oil

1 tablespoon fresh lemon juice

1 tablespoon minced shallot

1 teaspoon green peppercorns in brine
   (drained and rinsed), or more to taste
   (see Tip)

1 teaspoon Dijon mustard

Dash of salt, or to taste

To Complete the Recipe

8 ounces creste di gallo (about 3 cups)

4 ounces smoked salmon, cut into
   $1/2$-inch squares (remove and discard
   skin, then cut fish)

2 medium scallions, diagonally cut into
   thin slices

GARNISH (OPTIONAL) snipped fresh dill, sliced Niçoise olives

(continues)

1. Bring a large pot of water to a boil over high heat.

2. Meanwhile, process all of the sauce ingredients in a blender or food processor until smooth; set aside.

3. Add salt, then the creste di gallo to the boiling water. When the water returns to a boil, stir occasionally to separate the pasta. Reduce the heat to medium-high and cook for about 9 to 11 minutes, or according to package instructions, until noodles are *al dente*. Drain and rinse well in cold water, then drain again.

4. Transfer the pasta to a large bowl. Add the salmon and the scallions; toss gently. Add the vinaigrette and toss again. Adjust the seasoning to taste.

> ### TIP
>
> Green peppercorns are unripe pepper berries which, instead of being dried, are preserved in brine; rinse them and then crush or purée before using. They share the basic taste of dried pepper and also have their own sharp, almost acidic flavor.

PER SERVING: Cal 338/Prot 12.4g/Carb 44.2g/Fat 12.4g/Chol 6mg/Sod 259mg

ADVANCE PREPARATION   Covered and refrigerated, the vinaigrette will keep for up to 1 week in a tightly closed container in the refrigerator. Combine with hot, freshly cooked pasta and allow to come to room temperature; serve within 1 hour. Or cover and refrigerate the salad; serve within 2 days. Bring to room temperature before serving.

Variation

•   Substitute other cooked seafood for the smoked salmon, such as poached white fish or tuna, or use canned water-packed solid white albacore tuna (drained and flaked).

pasta salad
niçoise

Makes 6 servings

Because this sunny, Mediterranean-inspired salad does not require constant refrigeration, it's a good take-along salad for summer picnics. But any time of the year, this is one of my favorites to have in the refrigerator when I want a delicious and satisfying lunch or dinner in a hurry.

10 ounces rigatoni (about 4 cups)

Sun-Dried Tomato-Rosemary Vinaigrette

$1/2$ cup oil-packed chopped sun-dried tomatoes; drain and reserve oil

2 tablespoons extra-virgin olive oil (or use reserved oil from the sun-dried tomatoes)

2 tablespoons red wine vinegar

2 tablespoons capers, drained and rinsed (see Tip)

1 teaspoon Dijon mustard

2 teaspoons minced fresh rosemary (or $1/4$ teaspoon dried rosemary, crushed)

$1/4$ teaspoon pepper, or to taste

$1/4$ teaspoon salt, or to taste

To Complete the Recipe

$1/2$ pound thin green beans, cut into 2-inch-long pieces (about 2 cups)

1 (6-ounce) can water-packed solid white albacore tuna, drained and flaked

1 (6-ounce) jar marinated quartered artichoke hearts, drained

$1/2$ cup coarsely chopped red bell pepper

$1/2$ cup thinly sliced red onion

$1/4$ cup finely chopped flat-leaf parsley

(continues)

141

GARNISH (OPTIONAL)   freshly ground black pepper, crumbled feta cheese

1. Bring a large pot of water to a boil over high heat; add salt, then the rigatoni. When the water returns to a boil, stir occasionally to separate the rigatoni. Reduce the heat to medium-high and cook for about 12 to 14 minutes, or according to package instructions, until noodles are *al dente*.

2. While the rigatoni is cooking, whisk together the vinaigrette ingredients in a small bowl; set aside.

3. Put the green beans into a medium microwave-proof dish; add about 1/4 cup water. Cover and microwave on high for about 4 minutes or until crisp-tender. (Or cook the beans for about 4 minutes in a stovetop steamer.) Drain and rinse well in cold water, then drain again.

4. When the rigatoni is done, drain and rinse well in cold water, then drain again.

5. Transfer the rigatoni to a large bowl. Add the beans and the remaining ingredients; toss. Add the dressing and toss again. Adjust the seasonings to taste.

> ## TIP
>
> Capers are the unopened flower buds of a shrub native to the Mediterranean and parts of Asia. The buds are dried in the sun and then pickled in a vinegar brine. Capers come in several sizes; the largest have the strongest flavor. The smallest, called "nonpareil," are subtle in taste but are the most tender and most expensive. Capers should be rinsed before using to remove excess salt. Once opened, store in the refrigerator for up to 3 months.

PER SERVING: Cal 353/Prot 18.5g/Carb 56.7g/Fat 5.9g/Chol 5mg/Sod 280mg

ADVANCE PREPARATION   The vinaigrette will keep for up to 1 week in a tightly closed container in the refrigerator. Covered and refrigerated, the completed salad will keep for up to 2 days. Bring to room temperature before serving.

Variation

•   Substitute canned salmon for the tuna.

tarragon-walnut chicken salad

Makes 4 servings

The distinctive, seductive, nutty flavor and aroma of walnut oil is the essence of this salad.

7 ounces farfalle (bow tie pasta);
   (about 3 cups)

1 tablespoon olive oil

12 ounces boneless skinless chicken
   breast halves, cut into 3-inch-long by
   $1/2$-inch-wide strips

Dash of pepper, or to taste

Walnut Vinaigrette

$1/4$ cup red wine vinegar

3 tablespoons walnut oil, preferably
   roasted (see Tips)

2 tablespoons fresh lemon juice

2 teaspoons Dijon mustard

$1/4$ cup minced fresh flat-leaf parsley

1 tablespoon minced fresh tarragon (or
   1 teaspoon dried tarragon)

$1/8$ teaspoon pepper, or to taste

Dash of salt, or to taste

To Complete the Recipe

3 plum tomatoes, each cut into 6 wedges

2 medium scallions, coarsely chopped

8 leaves red-leaf lettuce

GARNISH (OPTIONAL)   freshly ground black pepper, toasted chopped walnuts

(continues)

143

1. Bring a large pot of water to a boil over high heat; add salt, then the farfalle. When the water returns to a boil, stir occasionally to separate the farfalle. Reduce the heat to medium-high and cook for about 12 to 14 minutes, or according to package instructions, until noodles are *al dente*.

2. While the farfalle is cooking, heat the olive oil in a medium nonstick skillet over medium-high heat. Add the chicken; cook, stirring occasionally, for about 5 to 6 minutes or until it is lightly browned and cooked through.

3. Whisk together the vinegar, walnut oil, lemon juice, and mustard in a small bowl; stir in the remaining vinaigrette ingredients. Set aside.

4. When the chicken is done, transfer it to a plate and lightly sprinkle with pepper; allow to cool.

5. When the farfalle is done, drain and rinse well in cold water, then drain again.

6. Transfer the farfalle to a large bowl. Add the chicken, tomatoes, and scallions; toss. Add the vinaigrette and toss again. Adjust the seasonings to taste.

7. Serve the chicken salad atop the lettuce leaves arranged on individual salad plates.

> **TIP**
>
> Walnuts contain 60 percent oil. The oil has a pleasant, nutty taste and is used mainly for salads rather than as a cooking medium. The flavor is powerful, so a little goes a long way. Read the labels; inexpensive nut oils are likely to be a blend containing only a small percent of nut oil. Like other nut oils, walnut oil turns rancid quickly at room temperature; it will keep for up to 3 months in the refrigerator.

PER SERVING: Cal 446/Prot 31.4g/Carb 41.5g/Fat 17.2g/Chol 65mg/Sod 65mg

ADVANCE PREPARATION   The vinaigrette will keep in a tightly covered container in the refrigerator for up to 2 days. The completed salad can be made early the day it is to be served; allow it to come to room temperature and assemble the plates with the lettuce leaves just before serving.

penne
with *zesty*
italian dressing

Makes 6 servings

Pasta is the only ingredient that needs cooking in this salad. The fresh vegetables are left raw and crunchy, making this salad an especially good choice for a hot summer day. Another plus: The salad can be prepared in advance for carefree summer entertaining. Serve this dish solo as a light lunch or as a dinnertime accompaniment to fish or chicken on the grill.

8 ounces penne (about 3 cups)

Zesty Italian Dressing

$^1/_4$ cup extra-virgin olive oil

$^1/_4$ cup white wine vinegar (see Tip)

1 tablespoon minced shallot

1 tablespoon minced fresh flat-leaf parsley

1 teaspoon minced fresh chives

1 teaspoon minced fresh oregano (or $^1/_4$ teaspoon dried oregano)

$^1/_2$ teaspoon pepper, or to taste

$^1/_2$ teaspoon salt, or to taste

$^1/_4$ teaspoon red pepper flakes, or to taste

Pinch of powdered mustard (see Tip)

To Complete the Recipe

2 plum tomatoes, cut into $^1/_2$-inch cubes

1 small cucumber, peeled, seeded, and coarsely chopped (about 1 cup)

$^1/_2$ yellow bell pepper, coarsely chopped

2 medium scallions, coarsely chopped

$^1/_2$ cup mozzarella cheese in $^1/_2$-inch cubes

GARNISH (OPTIONAL)   freshly ground black pepper, freshly grated Parmesan cheese

(continues)

1. Bring a large pot of water to a boil over high heat; add salt, then the penne. When the water returns to a boil, stir occasionally to separate the penne. Reduce the heat to medium-high and cook for about 12 to 14 minutes, or according to package instructions, until noodles are *al dente*.

2. While the penne is cooking, whisk together the dressing ingredients in a small bowl; set aside.

3. When the penne is done, drain and rinse well in cold water, then drain again.

4. Transfer the penne to a large bowl. Add the remaining ingredients; toss. Add the dressing and toss again. Adjust the seasonings to taste.

TIPS

- Wine vinegars are produced from the acetic fermentation of wine; they are mellow in flavor and retain the aroma of the wine from which they are made. The name "vinegar" comes from the French "vin aigre," which means sour wine.

- Powdered mustard is made from finely ground mustard seed; it can be stored in a dry, dark place for up to 6 months.

PER SERVING: Cal 283/Prot 9.8g/Carb 32.2g/Fat 12.1g/Chol 11mg/Sod 270mg

ADVANCE PREPARATION   If dried oregano is used, allow the dressing to stand for 15 to 30 minutes before serving; it will keep for up to 1 week in a tightly closed container in the refrigerator. If fresh oregano is used, the dressing will keep for up to 4 days. Covered and refrigerated, the completed salad will keep for up to 2 days. Bring to room temperature before serving.

Variation

- When tossing the salad, add about 8 ounces shelled, cooked shrimp.

tuscan salad
with balsamic
vinaigrette

Makes 6 servings

Balsamic Vinaigrette is a personal favorite I developed for my cookbook, The Complete Book of Dressings. *Here, the slightly sweet dressing complements the spicy flavor of arugula.*

Balsamic Vinaigrette

1/4 cup balsamic vinegar (see Tip)

3 tablespoons extra-virgin olive oil

2 tablespoons water

2 teaspoons minced fresh basil (or 1/2 teaspoon dried basil)

1 teaspoon Dijon mustard

1 teaspoon light brown sugar

1 teaspoon minced garlic

1/2 teaspoon pepper, or to taste

1/4 teaspoon salt, or to taste

To Complete the Recipe

8 ounces capellini (angel hair pasta)

1 (19-ounce) can cannellini beans, drained and rinsed (see Tip)

1 cup coarsely shredded stemmed arugula leaves

1/4 cup diced red bell pepper

1/4 cup minced fresh flat-leaf parsley

2 tablespoons minced shallot

GARNISH (OPTIONAL)   freshly ground black pepper, freshly grated Parmesan cheese

1. Bring a large pot of water to a boil over high heat.

2. Meanwhile, combine the vinaigrette ingredients in a small bowl; whisk until the brown sugar is dissolved. Set aside.

(continues)

3. When the water comes to a boil, add salt, then the capellini. When the water returns to a boil, stir occasionally to separate the capellini. Reduce the heat to medium-high and cook for about 3 to 4 minutes, or according to package instructions, until noodles are *al dente*. Drain and rinse well in cold water, then drain again.

4. Transfer the capellini to a large bowl. Add the remaining ingredients and toss. Add the vinaigrette; toss again. Adjust the seasonings to taste.

PER SERVING: Cal 287/Prot 8.7g/Carb 45.6g/Fat 7.8g/Chol 0mg/Sod 288mg

ADVANCE PREPARATION   If dried basil is used, the vinaigrette will keep for up to 1 week in a tightly closed container in the refrigerator; if fresh basil is used, it will keep for up to 4 days. Covered and refrigerated, the completed salad will keep for up to 2 days. Bring to room temperature before serving.

Variation

• Substitute stemmed spinach leaves for the arugula.

TIPS

• Balsamic vinegar (the Italian *aceto balsamico*) is an Italian red wine vinegar made by boiling the juice of white Trebbiano grapes in copper pots until it caramelizes. It is then aged for 3 to 30 years in barrels made from various woods (oak, chestnut, mulberry, and juniper), each adding a hint of its woody flavor. The result is a vinegar with a heavy, mellow, almost sweet flavor, and a dark color. Beware of cheap imitations made with cane sugar, vanilla, licorice, and caramel flavoring. It pays to read the labels! Store balsamic vinegar in a cool, dark place for up to 6 months after it has been opened.

• Cannellini beans are large, white Italian kidney beans. In supermarkets, they can be found with the canned beans or with the Italian products.

shells and shrimp
with curried
chutney dressing

This easily portable salad is made to order to take along on a summer picnic when its succulent flavors fill the bill. Just take care to keep it well chilled until serving time.

8 ounces medium (1/2- to 1-inch) pasta
shells (about 3 cups)

Curried Chutney Dressing

1 tablespoon canola or safflower oil

1/4 cup minced shallots

1 tablespoon curry powder

1/2 cup nonfat plain yogurt

1/4 cup mango chutney (see Tip)

1/4 teaspoon pepper, or to taste

1/8 teaspoon salt, or to taste

1/8 teaspoon cayenne, or to taste (see Tip)

To Complete the Recipe

4 ounces frozen cooked salad shrimp,
thawed

1/3 cup golden raisins (see Tip)

1/2 red bell pepper, finely chopped

2 medium scallions, finely chopped

GARNISH (OPTIONAL)   freshly ground black pepper, toasted sliced almonds

1. Bring a large pot of water to a boil over high heat; add salt, then the pasta shells. When the water returns to a boil, stir occasionally to separate the shells. Reduce the heat to medium-high and cook for about 9 to 11 minutes, or according to package instructions, until noodles are *al dente*.

(continues)

2. While the shells are cooking, prepare the dressing: Heat the oil in a small nonstick skillet over medium-high heat. Add the shallots; cook, stirring constantly, for about 3 minutes or until tender. Remove the pan from the heat; stir the curry powder into the hot oil. Combine the remaining dressing ingredients in a small bowl; stir in the curry mixture.

3. When the shells are done, drain and rinse well in cold water, then drain again.

4. Transfer the shells to a large bowl. Add the remaining ingredients; toss. Add the dressing and toss again. Adjust the seasonings to taste.

PER SERVING: Cal 379/Prot 15.3g/Carb 67.5g/Fat 5.3g/Chol 44mg/Sod 135mg

ADVANCE PREPARATION   Covered and refrigerated, the dressing will keep for up to 2 days. The completed salad can be made early the day it is to be served.

Variation

• For a vegetarian version, substitute 1 cup steamed, shelled green soybeans (available fresh or frozen in many Asian stores and some supermarkets) for the shrimp.

TIPS

• Chutney is a mixture of fruit and/or vegetables cooked with vinegar, sugar, and spices. Most often made with mango, chutney is found in most supermarkets; look for it shelved with either the condiments or dressings.

• Cayenne is the ground dried pod of the small, more pungent varieties of chili peppers. Use with caution, because it is very hot. Store it in a tightly closed container in the refrigerator.

• Both dark and golden seedless raisins are made from Thompson seedless grapes. The dark raisins are sun-dried for several weeks. Golden raisins are treated with sulphur dioxide to prevent them from darkening; and they are dried with artificial heat, which produces a moister, plumper raisin. Store all raisins at room temperature for several months or refrigerate them in a tightly sealed plastic bag or container for up to 1 year.

Fragrant Chinese Noodle Salad
(page 152)

fragrant
chinese
noodle salad

Makes 6 servings

Traditional Chinese recipes don't contain balsamic vinegar, an Italian staple; but the combination of ingredients in this spicy dressing is magical. Any time of the year, this makes a delicious side-dish salad.

Soy-Balsamic Vinaigrette

1/4 cup low-sodium soy sauce

2 tablespoons balsamic vinegar

2 tablespoons dark sesame oil

1 tablespoon toasted sesame seeds

1 teaspoon Chinese hot oil, or to taste (see Tip)

1/2 teaspoon sugar

Dash of salt, or to taste

To Complete the Recipe

8 ounces thin Chinese wheat-flour noodles

1 cup finely shredded carrots

GARNISH (OPTIONAL)   black sesame seeds, scallion curls (see Tip)

1. Bring a large pot of water to a boil over high heat.

2. Meanwhile, whisk together the vinaigrette ingredients in a small bowl; make certain the sugar is dissolved. Set aside.

3. Add the noodles to the pot of boiling water. When the water returns to a boil, stir occasionally to separate the noodles. Reduce the heat to medium-high and cook for about 3 to 4 minutes, or according to package instructions, until noodles are *al dente*.

4. When the noodles are done, drain and rinse well in cold water, then drain again.

5. Transfer the noodles to a large bowl. Toss in the carrots. Add the vinaigrette and toss again. Adjust the seasonings to taste.

PER SERVING: Cal 206/Prot 4.6g/Carb 34.6g/Fat 5.5g/Chol 0mg/Sod 381mg

ADVANCE PREPARATION   Covered and refrigerated, this salad will keep for up to 3 days.

TIPS

- Chinese hot oil, also called red oil, chili oil, or hot pepper oil, is available in Asian markets and in some supermarkets. It is made from hot red pepper extract added to vegetable oil and is used as a flavoring oil rather than as a cooking oil, especially in Szechuan and Hunan recipes. Refrigerate after opening.

- To make "scallion curls," slice the green parts of scallions very thinly lengthwise. Drop into a bowl of ice water; curls will form in about 10 to 15 minutes. Use as a garnish.

szechuan
bow-tie
salad

Makes 6 servings

Thanks to red pepper flakes and hot pepper sauce in the vinaigrette and strips of red bell pepper on bow tie pasta, this salad is as lively in appearance as it is in flavor.

12 ounces farfalle (bow tie pasta); (about
    5 cups)

2 cups broccoli florets

Hot Pepper Vinaigrette

1/3 cup canola or safflower oil

1/3 cup red wine vinegar

2 tablespoons toasted sesame seeds

2 tablespoons honey

2 teaspoons hot pepper sauce, or to taste

1 teaspoon minced garlic

1 teaspoon minced fresh ginger

Pinch of red pepper flakes, or to taste

Dash of ground white pepper, or to taste

To Complete the Recipe

1 red bell pepper, cut into 1/4-inch-wide
    lengthwise strips

3 medium scallions, cut into 1/2-inch-long
    pieces

GARNISH (OPTIONAL)   toasted pine nuts, fresh watercress leaves (see Tip)

1. Bring a large pot of water to a boil over high heat; add salt, then the farfalle. When the water returns to a boil, stir occasionally to separate the farfalle. Reduce the heat to medium-high and cook for about 12 to 14 minutes, or according to package instructions, until noodles are *al dente*.

2. While the farfalle is cooking, put the broccoli florets into a medium microwave-proof dish; add about ¼ cup water. Cover and microwave on high for about 4 minutes or until crisp-tender. (Or cook the broccoli for about 5 minutes in a stovetop steamer.) Drain and rinse well in cold water, then drain again.

3. Whisk together the vinaigrette ingredients in a small bowl.

4. When the farfalle is done, drain and rinse well in cold water, then drain again.

5. Transfer the farfalle to a large bowl. Add the broccoli, bell pepper, and scallions; toss. Add the vinaigrette and toss again. Adjust the seasonings to taste.

PER SERVING: Cal 378/Prot 8.8g/Carb 52.7g/Fat 14.7g/Chol 0mg/Sod 17mg

ADVANCE PREPARATION   Covered and refrigerated, the vinaigrette will keep for up to 1 week. Cover and refrigerate the completed salad for up to 2 days.

Variation

*   Substitute other vegetables for the broccoli (up to 3 cups total). Try steamed cut asparagus, blanched snow peas (see Tip), or sliced mushrooms.

> ## TIPS
>
> *   Watercress, a member of the mustard family, has small, crisp, dark green leaves that have a slightly bitter and peppery flavor. Refrigerate the leaves in a plastic bag (or with stems immersed in a glass of water covered with a plastic bag) for up to 5 days. Wash before using.
>
> *   "Blanching" means to plunge food quickly into simmering water and then immediately into cold water to stop the cooking. Blanching enhances the color and flavor of vegetables and also loosens the skins of tomatoes, peaches, and nuts (such as almonds), making them easy to peel.

green noodle-couscous
with spicy
peanut dressing

Makes 4 servings

This salad, adapted from my cookbook, The 15-Minute Single Gourmet, *is a favorite in my noodle cooking classes. The salad's character can be mild or zesty; simply adjust the heat by using the amount of red pepper flakes that suit your taste.*

4 ounces spinach ribbon noodles (about
   3 cups)

3/4 cup couscous (see Tip)

3/4 cup hot water

Spicy Peanut Dressing

1/3 cup smooth peanut butter

1/4 cup white rice vinegar

1/4 cup nonfat plain yogurt

1 tablespoon low-sodium soy sauce

1 teaspoon dark sesame oil

1 teaspoon minced garlic

1/2 teaspoon red pepper flakes, to taste

Dash of salt, or to taste

1 tablespoon water, or as needed

To Complete the Recipe

1/2 medium red bell pepper, coarsely
   chopped

2 medium scallions, thinly sliced

1/4 cup minced fresh flat-leaf parsley

GARNISH (OPTIONAL)   mandarin orange segments or pineapple chunks, sprigs of fresh cilantro or flat-leaf parsley

1. Bring a large pot of water to a boil over high heat; add salt, then the noodles. When the water returns to a boil, stir occasionally to separate the noodles. Reduce the heat to medium-high and and cook for about 5 to 7 minutes, or according to package instructions, until noodles are *al dente*.

2. While the noodles are cooking, combine the couscous and hot water in a small bowl. Cover and let stand for about 5 minutes or until the liquid is completely absorbed.

3. Whisk together the dressing ingredients, except the water, in a small bowl. The dressing should have a cake-batter consistency; add water as needed. Set aside.

4. When the noodles are done, drain and rinse well in cold water, then drain again. Fluff the couscous with a fork.

5. Combine the bell pepper, scallions, and parsley in a large bowl. Add the noodles and couscous; toss. Add the dressing and toss again. Adjust the seasonings to taste.

PER SERVING: Cal 386/Prot 14.6g/Carb 54.2g/Fat 12.3g/Chol 0mg/Sod 268mg

ADVANCE PREPARATION   This salad is ideal for advance preparation. Toss the salad ingredients and prepare the dressing up to 1 day in advance; cover and refrigerate separately. Toss the salad with the dressing just before serving.

> ### TIP
>
> Couscous, sometimes called Moroccan pasta, is a tiny, beadlike pasta made from semolina flour. It is available in both white and whole wheat varieties in most supermarkets, usually in the rice aisle. Couscous keeps almost indefinitely in a tightly closed container in a dark, dry place. This quick-cooking pasta is prepared by combining equal amounts of couscous and hot (nearly boiling) liquid, such as water, chicken broth, or vegetable stock. Then, simply let it stand in a covered bowl for about 5 to 10 minutes or until the couscous is tender and the liquid is completely absorbed. (Couscous will double in volume as it absorbs the liquid.) Before serving, fluff with a fork.

layered spinach-noodle salad with lime-ginger dressing

Makes 4 servings

If time permits, top the layers of crunchy vegetables with grilled fresh tuna rather than using canned tuna. Or if you prefer, transform this into a colorful vegetarian salad—just omit the tuna entirely.

8 ounces spinach egg noodles

Lime-Ginger Dressing

$^1/_3$ cup fresh lime juice

$^1/_3$ cup low-sodium soy sauce

2 tablespoons canola or safflower oil

2 teaspoons minced fresh ginger

1 teaspoon minced garlic

$^1/_2$ teaspoon sugar

Dash of ground white pepper, or to taste

To Complete the Recipe

1 red bell pepper, coarsely chopped

$^1/_2$ yellow bell pepper, coarsely chopped

2 medium scallions, coarsely chopped

6 cups coarsely shredded stemmed spinach leaves (about 6 ounces)

1 (6-ounce) can water-packed solid white albacore tuna, drained and flaked (see Tips)

GARNISH (OPTIONAL)   toasted pine nuts

1. Bring a large pot of water to a boil over high heat; add salt, then the noodles. When the water returns to a boil, stir occasionally to separate the noodles. Reduce the heat to

medium-high and cook for about 8 to 10 minutes, or according to package instructions, until noodles are *al dente.*

2. While the noodles are cooking, whisk together the dressing ingredients in a small bowl; set aside. Toss together the bell peppers and scallions in a small bowl; set aside.

3. When the noodles are done, drain and rinse well in cold water, then drain again.

4. Transfer the noodles to a medium bowl. Add ¼ cup of the dressing and toss. Adjust the seasoning to taste.

5. To assemble, layer the ingredients on individual salad plates as follows: spinach, noodles, bell pepper mixture, tuna. Drizzle each salad with about 2 tablespoons of the remaining dressing.

PER SERVING: Cal 391/Prot 24.8g/Carb 54.2g/Fat 8.3g/Chol 18mg/Sod 967mg

ADVANCE PREPARATION   Covered and refrigerated, the dressing will keep for up to 2 days. The noodles can be tossed with dressing, and the bell pepper mixture can be prepared early the day the salad is to be served; cover and refrigerate the separate components. To use, bring to room temperature and assemble the salads just before serving.

Variations

- Substitute wide egg noodles for the spinach egg noodles.

- Rather than layering the salad ingredients, toss them together with all of the dressing.

TIPS

When buying canned tuna, read the labels:

- Oil-packed tuna is usually packed in low-grade vegetable oil, so tuna packed in spring water is not only lower in calories but also has a better flavor.

- Solid-pack tuna is a continuous piece of tuna, more expensive than chunk or flaked, but better in flavor and texture.

- Solid-pack tuna comes in three grades: white (albacore), light, and dark meat. Canned albacore tuna is the most expensive but is preferable for its mild flavor and appearance.

- The salt in canned tuna (as well as other canned foods) can be reduced by rinsing the fish under cool running tap water for 1 minute.

thai
cellophane noodles
with **shrimp**

Makes 4 servings

Freshly cooked cocktail shrimp are available in many supermarket seafood departments; if you prefer, substitute them for the smaller frozen cooked salad shrimp. Both work well to add color and taste to this satisfying salad. Plan ahead when serving this salad; the enticing marriage of spicy and nutty flavors is best if allowed to develop for several hours before mealtime.

4 ounces thin cellophane noodles

Peanut-Ginger Dressing

$1/2$ cup unsalted dry-roasted peanuts

1 piece fresh ginger, 2-inches long by 1-inch thick, peeled and cut into $1/2$-inch-thick chunks (or 2 tablespoons minced fresh ginger)

1 teaspoon minced hot red chili pepper (seeds removed), or to taste (see Tips)

$1/4$ cup fresh lime juice

2 tablespoons low-sodium soy sauce

2 tablespoons sugar

To Complete the Recipe

8 ounces frozen cooked salad shrimp, thawed

2 tablespoons diced red bell pepper

2 tablespoons chopped fresh basil (fresh is essential)

GARNISH (OPTIONAL)   sprigs of fresh basil or cilantro

1. Bring a medium saucepan of water to a boil over high heat; remove from the heat. Add the cellophane noodles; soak, stirring occasionally, for about 8 to 10 minutes, or according to package instructions, until noodles are softened and clear. (If the noodles are thick, it may be necessary to cook them in boiling water.)

2. While the noodles are soaking, put all of the dressing ingredients into a food processor or electric mincer; process until the ginger is finely chopped and the peanuts are slightly chunky.

3. When the noodles are softened and clear, drain and rinse well in cold water, then drain again. Rinse with cool water and drain again.

4. Transfer the noodles to a large bowl; use kitchen shears to cut them into about 6-inch lengths. Add the dressing and toss. Add the remaining ingredients; toss again. Adjust the amount of hot chili pepper to taste.

PER SERVING: Cal 241/Prot 12g/Carb 26.3g/Fat 9.8g/Chol 108mg/Sod 482mg

ADVANCE PREPARATION   This salad should stand at room temperature for about $1/2$ hour before serving; or cover and refrigerate for up to 8 hours.

Variations

• Substitute about $1/2$ teaspoon red pepper flakes or about 1 teaspoon chili paste with garlic for the fresh hot red chili pepper.

• For a milder flavor, substitute green chili pepper or jalapeño pepper for the hot red chili pepper.

• Substitute fresh cilantro or mint for the basil.

• Substitute fresh lemon juice or white rice vinegar for the lime juice.

TIPS

• Just how hot a pepper is depends on the amount it contains of a substance called capsaicin (kap-SAY-ih-sihn), found mainly in the veins near the seeds. Unaffected by heat or cold, capsaicin retains its potency despite time, cooking, or freezing, so removing the membranes and seeds before using peppers is the only way to reduce the heat. Small peppers have more membranes and seeds than large peppers, so generally they are hotter.

• To avoid irritation from the caustic oils in chili peppers, do not touch your eyes, nose, or lips while handling them. Many cooks wear disposable plastic gloves when working with hot chilies. Afterward, wash your hands, knife, and cutting board in hot, soapy water.

chapter 3 *Chilled Noodles*

asparagus-ramen salad
with sesame-soy
vinaigrette

Makes 4 servings

When the first asparagus appears in spring, I celebrate its return with this light salad. If company's coming, arrange each serving individually with a touch of artistry. For a more substantial entrée salad, top the servings with grilled teriyaki salmon steaks or shrimp.

6 ounces baked ramen noodles

3 cups asparagus in 2-inch-long pieces,
   diagonally cut (see Tips)

Sesame-Soy Vinaigrette

1/4 cup low-sodium soy sauce

2 tablespoons canola or safflower oil

2 tablespoons white rice vinegar

2 teaspoons dark sesame oil

1 teaspoon minced garlic

1 teaspoon sugar

1/8 teaspoon red pepper flakes, or to taste

To Complete the Recipe

1/2 red bell pepper, cut into 2-inch-long by
   1/4-inch-wide strips

GARNISH (OPTIONAL)   toasted sesame seeds

1. Bring a medium pot of water to a boil over high heat; drop in the noodles. Reduce the heat to medium-high and cook for about 3 to 4 minutes, or according to package instructions, until noodles are *al dente*. As the noodles cook, stir occasionally with a fork to separate.

2. While the noodles are cooking, put the asparagus into a medium microwave-proof dish; add about ¼ cup water. Cover and microwave on high for about 4 minutes or until crisp-tender. (Or cook the asparagus for about 5 minutes in a stovetop steamer.) Drain and rinse well in cold water, then drain again.

3. Combine the dressing ingredients in a small bowl; whisk until the sugar is dissolved. Adjust the seasoning to taste.

4. When the noodles are done, drain and rinse well in cold water, then drain again. Transfer them to a large bowl; add ¼ cup of the dressing and toss.

5. To assemble the salads, divide the noodles among four shallow bowls. Top with the asparagus and red pepper strips. Drizzle each serving with 1 tablespoon of the remaining dressing.

PER SERVING: Cal 307/Prot 18.6g/Carb 44.1g/Fat 10.7g/Chol 0mg/Sod 723mg

ADVANCE PREPARATION   Covered and refrigerated, the vinaigrette will keep for up to 1 week. Prepare the other ingredients and assemble the salads just before serving.

Variation

• Rather than layering the salad ingredients, toss them together with all of the vinaigrette.

> ## TIPS
>
> • Asparagus is at its best in the early spring. Choose green spears with firm stalks; the tips should be tightly closed and have a lavender hue. Slender stalks are more tender. Thick stalks can be halved lengthwise or peeled; they are usually the better choice for diagonal cutting.
>
> • To store, wrap asparagus in a plastic bag and store in the vegetable crisper; use within 2 to 3 days. Do not clean the asparagus until you are ready to cook it. If wilted, stand the stalks in a jar filled with 2 inches of very cold water. Cover with a plastic bag, seal, and refrigerate for 1 to 2 hours before cooking.

chicken stir-fry salad
with *zesty*
orange dressing

Makes 4 servings

Chinese wheat-flour noodles tossed with Zesty Orange Dressing form a delectable foundation for a warm dish of stir-fried vegetables and chicken. If you wish, prepare the stir-fry and noodles in advance; later the same day, serve both at room temperature atop a layer of shredded romaine lettuce, salad spinach leaves, or mesclun (see Tip).

Zesty Orange Dressing

1 teaspoon orange zest

1/2 cup fresh orange juice

1 tablespoon canola or safflower oil

2 teaspoons sugar

1 tablespoon low-sodium soy sauce

2 teaspoons dark sesame oil

1 teaspoon toasted sesame seeds

1/8 teaspoon pepper, or to taste

To Complete the Recipe

1 tablespoon canola or safflower oil

12 ounces boneless skinless chicken
    breast halves, cut into 2-inch-long by
    1/2-inch-wide strips

4 cups asparagus in 2-inch-long pieces

1/2 red bell pepper, cut into 2-inch-long by
    1/4-inch-wide strips

2 medium scallions, coarsely chopped

1 teaspoon minced garlic

8 ounces thin Chinese wheat-flour noodles

GARNISH (OPTIONAL)   freshly ground black pepper, toasted sesame seeds, orange slices

1. Bring a large pot of water to a boil over high heat.

2. Meanwhile, combine the dressing ingredients in a small bowl; whisk until the sugar is dissolved. Adjust the seasoning to taste; set aside.

3. Heat the canola or safflower oil in a large nonstick skillet over medium-high heat. Add the chicken, asparagus, and bell pepper; stir-fry for about 5 minutes. Add the scallions and garlic; stir-fry for about 1 more minute. The chicken should be lightly browned and cooked through, the asparagus crisp-tender. Reduce the heat to low. Whisk the dressing; add about 1/4 cup to the stir-fried mixture and stir gently until warm (the vinaigrette will evaporate if permitted to boil).

4. While the chicken and vegetables are cooking, add the noodles to the pot of boiling water. When the water returns to a boil, stir occasionally to separate the noodles. Reduce the heat to medium and cook for about 3 to 5 minutes, or according to package instructions, until noodles are *al dente*. Drain and rinse well in cold water, then drain again.

5. Transfer the noodles to a medium bowl; add the remaining dressing and toss.

6. To serve, divide the noodles among four plates; top with the warm stir-fried chicken and vegetables or allow to come to room temperature before serving.

PER SERVING: Cal 492/Prot 35.2g/Carb 60.3g/Fat 12.3g/Chol 65mg/Sod 204mg

ADVANCE PREPARATION   The dressing will keep for up to 2 days in a tightly closed container in the refrigerator. The noodles, as well as the stir-fried chicken and vegetables, can be prepared and combined with the vinaigrette early the day they are to be served; cover and refrigerate separately. Allow the components to come to room temperature and assemble the salads just before serving.

Variation

• When stir-frying, substitute other vegetables for the asparagus and bell pepper (up to 5 cups total). Try thin carrot strips, small broccoli florets, or snow peas.

TIP

Mesclun is a salad mix found in specialty produce markets and most supermarkets. It is a mixture of young, tender salad greens with flavors ranging from peppery to bitter or sweet; it may include arugula, frisée, mizuna, baby spinach, oak leaf, radicchio, sorrell, or any combination of these. If refrigerated in a plastic bag, it will keep for up to 5 days. Wash and gently pat dry before using.

chinese noodles
with spicy
sesame-pepper dressing

Makes 4 servings

This spicy noodle side dish is equally intriguing served chilled, at room temperature, or warm.
I like to partner it with teriyaki grilled chicken.

4 ounces thin Chinese wheat-flour noodles

Spicy Sesame-Pepper Dressing

2 tablespoons low-sodium soy sauce

2 tablespoons white rice vinegar

1 tablespoon dark sesame oil

$1/4$ teaspoon red pepper flakes, or to taste
(see Tip)

$1/8$ teaspoon pepper, or to taste

GARNISH (OPTIONAL)   toasted sesame seeds or black sesame seeds (see Tips)

1. Bring a medium saucepan of water to a boil over high heat; add the noodles. When the water returns to a boil, stir occasionally to separate the noodles. Reduce the heat to medium-high and cook for about 3 to 5 minutes, or according to package instructions, until noodles are *al dente.*

2. While the noodles are cooking, whisk together the dressing ingredients in a small bowl.

3. When the noodles are done, drain well; return to the pot. Whisk the dressing again, add it to the noodles, and toss. Adjust the seasonings to taste. Serve warm, allow to come to room temperature, or cover and refrigerate.

PER SERVING: Cal 134/Prot 3.3g/Carb 21.5g/Fat 3.9g/Chol 0mg/Sod 613mg

ADVANCE PREPARATION   The dressing will keep for up to 1 week in a tightly closed container in the refrigerator. Covered and refrigerated, the completed dish will keep for up to 2 days.

Variation

- Add vegetables (up to 1 cup) such as shredded carrots, diced cucumber, or diced red bell pepper.

TIPS

- Red pepper flakes, also called crushed red pepper, are the seeds and flakes of fiery hot peppers—a small amount goes a long way! Refrigerate to preserve the color and flavor.

- Sesame seeds come in shades of brown, red, and black. The most common are an ivory color; they are sold both with or without their brownish-gray hulls. Because they contain oil, all sesame seeds will become rancid at room temperature; store them in an airtight container in the refrigerator for up to 6 months or in the freezer for up to 1 year.

- To toast sesame seeds, put them in a dry nonstick skillet over medium-high heat for 3 to 5 minutes. Toss constantly and watch closely; immediately remove the seeds from the pan when they become lightly browned. As an alternative, spread the seeds on an ungreased baking sheet and bake in a 350°F oven. Shake the pan or stir occasionally for about 10 minutes or until the seeds are lightly browned. Either method will give the seeds a nutty flavor and a slightly crispy texture. It takes the same amount of time to toast 1 tablespoon or $1/2$ cup—so toast extra seeds, store them in an airtight container, and refrigerate or freeze.

spicy
cellophane noodles
with **scallops**

Makes 6 servings

My friend Nathan Fong, an award-winning food stylist and cooking instructor, shared several of his favorite chilled noodle recipes with me. I adapted this delicious recipe for the 15-minute cook., but you do need to plan ahead in order to marinate the scallops.

Spicy Soy-Lime Dressing

3 tablespoons low-sodium soy sauce

1 teaspoon lime zest

2 tablespoons fresh lime juice

1 tablespoon canola or safflower oil

1 tablespoon dark sesame oil

1 tablespoon white rice vinegar

1 tablespoon chili paste with garlic, or to taste

1 tablespoon honey

1 teaspoon Asian fish sauce, or to taste (see Tip)

1 teaspoon minced fresh ginger

1/4 teaspoon salt, or to taste

Dash of ground white pepper, or to taste

To Complete the Recipe

1 pound sea scallops (about 18); (see Tip)

4 ounces thin cellophane noodles

1 red bell pepper, diced

1/2 cup toasted raw cashews, coarsely chopped

1 medium scallion, minced

1/4 cup coarsely chopped fresh mint (fresh is essential)

1/4 cup coarsely chopped fresh cilantro (fresh is essential)

GARNISH (OPTIONAL)   sprigs of fresh mint or cilantro

1. Whisk together the dressing ingredients in a small bowl; set aside.

2. Rinse the scallops with cool water; drain well. Pour $^1/_4$ cup of the dressing over the scallops in a small bowl; stir gently. Cover and refrigerate for about 30 minutes to 2 hours.

3. While the scallops are marinating, bring a medium saucepan of water to a boil over high heat; remove from the heat. Add the cellophane noodles and soak for about 8 to 10 minutes, stirring occasionally, or according to package instructions, until noodles are softened and clear. (If the noodles are thick, it may be necessary to cook them in boiling water.) Drain and rinse well in cold water, then drain again.

4. Transfer the noodles to a large bowl; use kitchen shears to cut them into about 6-inch lengths. Add the remaining dressing and toss. Add the remaining ingredients; toss again. Adjust the seasonings to taste. Cover and set aside.

5. When you are ready to cook the scallops, place the oven rack 4 to 5 inches from the heating element and preheat the oven broiler. Use a slotted spoon to transfer the scallops to a shallow pan. (Discard the remaining marinade.) Broil the scallops for 2 to 4 minutes, turning once, until they are cooked through. Transfer to a plate and allow to cool.

6. To serve, arrange the scallops over the noodles on salad plates.

PER SERVING: Cal 268/Prot 15.8g/Carb 26.8g/Fat 10.9g/Chol 25mg/Sod 492mg

TIPS

- Asian fish sauce (*nuoc nam* on Vietnamese labels) refers to several mixtures based on the liquid from salted, fermented fish. The sauce which is found in Asian markets, is pungent and strong-flavored and the saltiness varies; use it in moderation and then add more to taste. After using, tightly close the container and refrigerate for up to 1 year.

- Sea scallops average $1^1/_2$ inches in diameter and should be pale beige to creamy pink in color; bay scallops are very tiny, about $^1/_2$ inch in diameter, and are sweeter in flavor. When buying fresh scallops, be certain that they have been refrigerated and that they are mild-smelling and firm in texture. Store the package in the coldest part of the refrigerator and use within 1 day of purchase. Before cooking, rinse under cool water and pat dry. Overcooking results in a tough, rubbery texture with little flavor; cook only until scallops are firm with opaque and white centers.

firecracker
noodles

Makes 6 servings

This is one of my friend Nathan's favorite chilled noodle recipes, and it has become one of mine, too. Its ingredient list has been pared down a bit, but the blend of Asian ingredients remains aromatic and zesty. I like to serve mounds of the noodles at room temperature on beds of shredded romaine lettuce, salad spinach leaves, or Chinese cabbage. For a touch of green, I garnish the plates with sprigs of fresh cilantro and blanched snow peas.

Spicy Pickled Ginger Vinaigrette

2 tablespoons low-sodium soy sauce

2 tablespoons white rice vinegar

1 tablespoon peanut oil, preferably roasted peanut oil

1 tablespoon dark sesame oil

1 tablespoon chili paste with garlic, or to taste

1 tablespoon fresh lemon juice

1 tablespoon honey

1 teaspoon minced pickled ginger (see Tip)

1/4 teaspoon salt, or to taste

To Complete the Recipe

8 ounces thin Chinese egg noodles

1 cup finely shredded carrot

2 medium scallions, diagonally cut into thin slices

1/2 cup finely chopped unsalted dry-roasted peanuts

1/4 cup chopped fresh cilantro

GARNISH (OPTIONAL)   black sesame seeds, sprigs of fresh cilantro, blanched snow peas

170

1. Bring a large pot of water to a boil over high heat.

2. Meanwhile, whisk together the dressing ingredients in a small bowl; set aside.

3. When the water comes to a boil, add the noodles. Reduce the heat to medium-high and cook for about 3 to 5 minutes, or according to package instructions, until noodles are *al dente*. As the noodles cook, stir occasionally with a fork to separate. Drain and rinse well in cold water, then drain again.

4. Transfer the noodles to a large bowl. Whisk the dressing; add to the noodles and toss. Let stand for about 10 minutes. Add the remaining ingredients and toss. Adjust the seasonings to taste.

PER SERVING: Cal 335/Prot 7.6g/Carb 29.7g/Fat 20.7g/Chol 0mg/Sod 808mg

ADVANCE PREPARATION   Covered and refrigerated, this salad will keep for up to 3 days. Bring to room temperature before serving.

Variation

- Substitute coarsely chopped fresh mint for the cilantro, or add 2 table-spoons coarsely chopped fresh mint in addition to the cilantro.

TIP

Pickled ginger is a cool, sharp condiment made from young ginger that have been marinated in seasoned vinegar. It is available in jars in Asian markets and some supermarkets. Pickled ginger is often used as a garnish for Asian dishes and is eaten in small bites to cleanse the palate, as when it is served with sushi.

chinese
chicken salad
with sesame-ginger dressing

Makes 4 servings

"Chicken salad" can be much more than cubes of chicken tossed with bits of celery and smothered in mayonnaise! With the addition of noodles and Asian vegetables, it can become the star of a special meal. Here's a do-ahead entrée as gorgeous as it is delicious, with little mess to clean up after serving.

Sesame-Ginger Dressing

1/3 cup white rice vinegar

2 tablespoons low-sodium soy sauce

1 tablespoon dark sesame oil

1 teaspoon finely minced fresh ginger

2 teaspoons sugar

1 teaspoon minced garlic

1 teaspoon toasted sesame seeds

Dash of ground white pepper, or to taste

To Complete the Recipe

12 ounces boneless skinless chicken
   breast halves

6 ounces baked ramen noodles

2 cups coarsely shredded Chinese cabbage

3 ribs bok choy, diagonally cut into
   1/4-inch-thick slices; also shred
   green tops

3 medium scallions, coarsely chopped

1/2 cup coarsely shredded carrot (see Tip)

1 (8-ounce) can mandarin orange
   segments, drained

GARNISH (OPTIONAL)   toasted pine nuts or toasted sesame seeds

1. Bring a medium saucepan of water to a boil over high heat.

2. At the same time, pour water into a medium sauté pan, to a level of about $1^{1}/_{2}$-inches deep; stir in a dash of salt and bring to a boil over high heat.

3. Meanwhile, combine the dressing ingredients in a small bowl; whisk until the sugar is dissolved. Adjust the seasoning to taste; set aside.

4. Add the chicken to the sauté pan (it should be covered by about 1/2 inch of water). Reduce heat to medium; cover and simmer for about 8 to 10 minutes or until the chicken is just cooked through.

5. While the chicken is cooking, drop the noodles into the saucepan of boiling water. When the water returns to a boil, reduce the heat to medium-high and cook for about 3 to 4 minutes, or according to package instructions, until noodles are *al dente*. As the noodles cook, stir occasionally with a fork to separate. When the noodles are done, drain and rinse well in cold water, then drain again.

6. Transfer the noodles to a medium bowl; add 1/4 cup of the dressing and toss.

7. When the chicken is done, use a slotted spoon to transfer it to a plate. Cut the chicken into 2-inch-long by $^{1}/_{2}$-inch-wide strips and allow to cool. (Discard the poaching liquid.)

8. Toss together the Chinese cabbage, bok choy, scallions, carrot, and chicken strips in a large bowl; add the remaining dressing and toss again.

9. To serve, divide and spread noodles among 4 plates; top with the chicken mixture. Garnish with the mandarin oranges.

> **TIP**
>
> The best carrots are young and slender; avoid buying carrots with cracks or root growth. If purchased with the greens attached, remove the greenery as soon as possible because it robs carrots of both vitamins and moisture. Store carrots in a plastic bag in the refrigerator's vegetable bin. However, do not store carrots near apples, which emit ethylene gas that turns carrots bitter.

PER SERVING: Cal 373/Prot 29.9g/Carb 46.8g/Fat 7.4g/Chol 65mg/Sod 512mg

ADVANCE PREPARATION   The dressing will keep for up to 2 weeks in a tightly closed container in the refrigerator. The chicken can be cooked early the day it is to be served; cover and refrigerate. Assemble the salads just before serving.

shrimp and pine-nut
lo mein

Makes 4 servings

For an out-of-the-ordinary twist that adds both intrigue and nutrition, garnish the servings with hijiki (see Tip); if you have never tasted these sea vegetables, you are in for a pleasant surprise.

6 ounces lo mein noodles	2 medium scallions, coarsely chopped
1/4 cup low-sodium soy sauce	1 pound medium shrimp (about 30), shelled and deveined
1 tablespoon dark sesame oil	
1/4 teaspoon red pepper flakes, or to taste	1/4 cup pine nuts
1 tablespoon canola or safflower oil	1 teaspoon minced garlic
3 cups sliced mushrooms	1 teaspoon minced fresh ginger

1. Bring a large pot of water to a boil over high heat; add the noodles. When the water returns to a boil, stir occasionally to separate the noodles. Reduce the heat to medium-high and cook for about 3 to 4 minutes, or according to package instructions, until noodles are *al dente*.

2. While the noodles are cooking, stir together the soy sauce, sesame oil, and red pepper flakes in a small bowl.

3. When the noodles are done, drain and rinse well in cold water, then drain again.

4. Transfer the noodles to a medium bowl and toss with 3 tablespoons of the soy sauce mixture; set aside.

5. Heat the oil in a large nonstick skillet over medium-high heat. Add the mushrooms and scallions. Cook, stirring occasionally, for about 5 minutes or until tender. Reduce the heat to medium. Add the shrimp, pine nuts, garlic, and ginger; cook, stirring constantly, for about 2 minutes or until the shrimp are cooked through and the pine nuts are lightly browned. Remove from the heat. Stir in the remaining soy sauce mixture. Adjust the seasoning to taste. Serve warm or allow to come to room temperature before serving.

6. To serve, transfer the noodles to individual bowls; top with the shrimp mixture.

PER SERVING: Cal 427/Prot 29.7g/Carb 43.1g/Fat 15.1g/Chol 175mg/Sod 744mg

ADVANCE PREPARATION   Covered and refrigerated, this dish will keep for up to 2 days. Bring to room temperature before serving.

Variation

• Hydrate 1 cup dry hijiki (see Tip); divide between the servings as a garnish atop the stir-fried shrimp mixture.

> ### TIP
>
> Hijiki (sometimes spelled "hiziki") is a dried black seaweed, or sea vegetable, with a slight anise flavor and high calcium content; it is found in Asian markets and in some supermarkets. To reconstitute before adding to recipes, put the hijiki strands into a bowl and cover with warm water; allow to stand until the hijiki begins to soften, about 15 minutes. Drain in a colander and rinse well. Transfer the hijiki to a small saucepan; cover with fresh water. Bring the water to a boil over high heat. Reduce the heat to medium-high and simmer until softened, about 15 to 20 minutes; drain well. Covered and refrigerated, the moistened hijiki will keep for up to 2 days. Add to stir-fries, soups, and salads.

chickpea-noodle salad
with ginger-soy
vinaigrette

Makes 4 servings

Pair this with a hearty bowl of steaming soup for winter fare or with a chilled soup for lunch or dinner on a hot summer day.

8 ounces thin Chinese wheat-flour noodles

Ginger-Soy Vinaigrette

1/4 cup white rice vinegar

2 tablespoons low-sodium soy sauce

1 tablespoon canola or safflower oil

1 tablespoon toasted sesame seeds

1 teaspoon Dijon mustard

1/2 teaspoon minced garlic

1/2 teaspoon minced fresh ginger

1/4 teaspoon pepper, or to taste

To Complete the Recipe

1 (15-ounce) can garbanzo beans, drained and rinsed (see Tip)

2 cups sliced mushrooms

2 medium scallions, finely chopped

1/2 cup diced red bell pepper

2 tablespoons minced fresh cilantro, or to taste (do not use dried cilantro; if fresh is unavailable, substitute 2 tablespoons minced fresh flat-leaf parsley)

4 large leaves red leaf lettuce

GARNISH (OPTIONAL) sprigs of fresh cilantro, red bell pepper strips

1. Bring a large pot of water to a boil over high heat; add the noodles. When the water returns to a boil, stir occasionally to separate the noodles. Reduce the heat to medium-high and cook for about 3 to 5 minutes, or according to package instructions, until noodles are *al dente*.

2. While the noodles are cooking, whisk together the vinaigrette ingredients in a small bowl; set aside.

3. When the noodles are done, drain and rinse well in cold water, then drain again. Transfer them to a large bowl and add the beans, mushrooms, scallions, bell pepper, and cilantro; toss. Add the vinaigrette and toss again. Adjust the seasoning to taste.

4. To serve, mound the noodle salad atop lettuce leaves on individual salad plates and garnish.

PER SERVING: Cal 167/Prot 6.8g/Carb 22g/Fat 5.8g/Chol 0mg/Sod 707mg

ADVANCE PREPARATION The vinaigrette will keep in a tightly covered container in the refrigerator for up to 1 week. Covered and refrigerated, the completed salad will keep for up to 2 days. Bring to room temperature before serving.

TIP

Garbanzo beans are sometimes called chickpeas, ceci beans, or Spanish beans. They are nut-like in flavor, and in appearance, too, for they have a shape and size similar to that of a hazelnut. Cooking dry garbanzo beans from scratch requires 8 hours of soaking and 3 hours of cooking. Canned garbanzo beans are the best alternative, their only disadvantage being the salt in the water in which they are canned; remove at least some of it by draining and rinsing the beans well before using.

crunchy
sweet-sour
ramen-cabbage salad

Makes 8 side dish servings

My friend, Marcia Nakashima Rogers, shared this recipe with me. It's one of her family's favorites, and it has become one of ours, too. Refrigerate the cabbage-vinaigrette mixture for at least 3 hours to allow the flavors to blend, then serve the refreshing salad chilled. In order to keep the noodles crunchy, it's important to add them just before serving.

Sweet-Sour Vinaigrette

1/2 cup rice wine vinegar or white rice vinegar

2 tablespoons low-sodium soy sauce

1 tablespoon dark sesame oil

1 tablespoon toasted sesame seeds

1 teaspoon sugar

To Complete the Recipe

4 cups finely shredded purple cabbage (see Tip)

1/2 cup scallions in 2-inch-long thin strips

4 ounces frozen cooked salad shrimp, thawed

3 ounces baked ramen noodles, broken (use right from the package without cooking)

1. Combine the vinaigrette ingredients together in a small bowl; whisk until the sugar is dissolved.

2. Toss together the cabbage, scallions, and shrimp in a medium bowl. Add the vinaigrette and toss again. Cover and refrigerate for 3 to 4 hours.

3. When ready to serve, toss with the noodles and serve chilled.

PER SERVING: Cal 90/Prot 3.1g/Carb 13.1g/Fat 2.8g/Chol 7mg/Sod 265mg

ADVANCE PREPARATION   Covered and refrigerated, this salad will keep for up to 2 days. Add the ramen noodles just before serving.

Variations

• Add 2 tablespoons coarsely chopped pickled ginger to the vinaigrette.

• Omit the shrimp.

• Poach about 8 ounces boneless skinless chicken breasts in chicken broth; cool and shred. Substitute for the shrimp.

TIPS

• Cabbage is commonly available in compact heads ranging in color from almost white to green to purple. Choose a heavy head with fresh, crisp-looking leaves. Tightly wrapped and refrigerated, it will keep for up to 1 week.

• Shredding means to cut food into narrow strips. This can be done by hand with a sharp knife or a grater; or it can be accomplished more quickly by using a food processor fitted with a shredding disk.

udon noodles
with mango
in **ginger-chili sauce**

Makes 4 servings

East meets west in this best-of-best-worlds salad. If fresh mango is unavailable, substitute steamed asparagus or carrots. For vegetarians, the salad is delicious minus the scallops; just add more mango or vegetables.

8 ounces udon noodles

Ginger-Chili Sauce

2 tablespoons balsamic vinegar

2 tablespoons low-sodium soy sauce

2 tablespoons dark sesame oil

1 teaspoon chili paste with garlic, or to taste

1 teaspoon toasted sesame seeds

$^1/_2$ teaspoon minced fresh ginger

$^1/_2$ teaspoon sugar

To Complete the Recipe

1 tablespoon canola or safflower oil

10 ounces sea scallops (about 12); (halve if very large)

1 mango, peeled, seeded, and cut into 1-inch chunks (see Tips)

$^1/_2$ red bell pepper, finely chopped

2 medium scallions, diagonally cut into thin slices

GARNISH (OPTIONAL)   toasted sesame seeds

1. Bring a large pot of water to a boil over high heat; add the noodles. When the water returns to a boil, stir occasionally to separate the noodles. Reduce the heat to

medium-high and cook for about 7 to 9 minutes, or according to package instructions, until noodles are *al dente*.

2. While the noodles are cooking, combine the sauce ingredients in a medium bowl; whisk until the sugar is dissolved. Adjust the seasoning to taste; set aside.

3. Heat the canola or safflower oil in a medium nonstick skillet over medium heat. Add the scallops; cook, stirring occasionally, for about 2 to 3 minutes or just until they are firm with opaque and white centers. Use a slotted spoon to transfer them to a medium bowl; allow to cool.

4. When the noodles are done, drain and rinse well in cold water, then drain again.

5. Transfer the noodles to a large bowl. Add 2 tablespoons of the sauce and toss; set aside to cool.

6. Add the mango, bell pepper, and scallions to the scallops; toss. Add the remaining sauce and toss again.

7. To serve, divide the noodles among four salad plates; top with the scallop mixture.

PER SERVING: Cal 409/Prot 21.3g/Carb 52.6g/Fat 12.6g/Chol 23mg/Sod 1091mg

ADVANCE PREPARATION   Covered and refrigerated, this salad will keep for up to 1 day.

TIPS

- The color of a mango is unimportant—it may be green, orange, yellow, or red. Texture does matter—the mango should yield slightly to pressure when squeezed. To ripen, place the mango in a paper bag at room temperature for 1 or 2 days and check daily; black spots indicate over-ripe fruit. Once ripened, a mango will keep 2 to 3 days in the refrigerator. (However, the flavor is at its best served at room temperature.)

- The simplest method to cut a mango is to hold the mango horizontally; cut it in two lengthwise, slightly off-center, so the knife just misses the pit. Repeat the cut on the other side so a thin layer of flesh remains around the flat pit. Holding a half in the palm of your hand, slash the flesh into a lattice, cutting down to, but not through, the peel. Holding the mango flesh upward, carefully push the center of the peel with your thumbs to turn it inside out, opening the cuts of the flesh. Then cut the mango cubes from the peel.

harasume
noodle salad

Makes 8 servings

This colorful salad makes a great impression when served on a large platter, so it makes a perfect choice as a side-dish salad when entertaining a large group. Provide tongs for your guests to serve themselves. The choice of vegetables is almost limitless; choose a variety of colors and arrange them attractively on a large platter.

4 ounces thin cellophane noodles

Soy Sauce Dressing

$^{1}/_{3}$ cup white rice vinegar

$^{1}/_{4}$ cup low-sodium soy sauce (see Tip)

2 tablespoons dark sesame oil

1 tablespoon honey

Pinch of red pepper flakes, or to taste

To Complete the Recipe

1 tablespoon canola or safflower oil

2 eggs, lightly beaten

1 cup stemmed snow peas, blanched

1 cup sliced mushrooms

1 tomato, cut into 16 wedges

$^{1}/_{2}$ cucumber, cut into 2-inch-long by $^{1}/_{4}$-inch-wide strips

$^{1}/_{2}$ red bell pepper, cut into 2-inch-long by $^{1}/_{4}$-inch-wide strips

1 medium scallion, cut into 2-inch-long thin strips

1. Bring a medium saucepan of water to a boil over high heat; remove from the heat. Add the cellophane noodles and soak, stirring occasionally for about 8 to 10 minutes, or

according to package instructions, until noodles are softened and clear. (If the noodles are thick, it may be necessary to cook them in boiling water.)

2. While the noodles are soaking, whisk together the dressing ingredients in a small bowl; set aside. Adjust the seasoning to taste after the red pepper flakes are moistened.

3. Heat the canola or safflower oil in a small nonstick skillet over medium-high heat; add the eggs. As the edges become firm, use a spatula to push them toward the center without cutting through so the uncooked portions can reach the hot pan surface. Cook only until no uncooked egg remains, then slide the cooked eggs onto a plate. When cool, cut the eggs into 2-inch-long by $^1/_2$-inch-wide strips.

4. When the noodles are softened, drain and rinse well in cold water, then drain again. Transfer the noodles to a medium bowl. Use kitchen shears to cut them into about 6-inch lengths. Add 2 tablespoons of the dressing and toss gently. Spread the noodles evenly on a large round serving platter.

5. Arrange the eggs and vegetables pinwheel fashion over the noodles. (If a rectangular platter is used, arrange the eggs and vegetables in clumps.) For the most attractive appearance, take into account the colors when placing the vegetables; for example, position light-colored mushrooms between green snow peas and red bell pepper strips.

6. Pour the dressing over the salad just before serving.

PER SERVING: Cal 153/Prot 3.6g/Carb 19.8g/Fat 6.6g/Chol 53mg/Sod 298mg

ADVANCE PREPARATION   Covered and refrigerated, the dressing will keep for up to 1 week. The vegetables can be chopped up to 1 day in advance; cover tightly and refrigerate. Prepare the noodles and assemble the salad just before serving.

> ### TIP
>
> Low-sodium or "lite" soy sauce contains less sodium than traditional soy sauce or tamari, but it provides nearly the same flavor. Soy sauce will keep almost indefinitely if refrigerated.

Variation

•   Substitute other vegetables for the ones in the ingredient list (up to about 6 cups total). Try strips of jicama, celery, or zucchini, or steamed asparagus spears, broccoli florets, or carrot strips.

soba and cucumbers
with ginger-plum vinaigrette

Makes 6 servings

When cucumbers fill the garden, this refreshing salad makes a lovely light summer side dish. To serve the noodle mixture as an entrée, ideal for lunch on the patio, save about ¹/₄ cup of the vinaigrette when tossing the salad. Top portions with chilled grilled shrimp and drizzle with the reserved vinaigrette.

8 ounces soba noodles

Ginger-Plum Vinaigrette

¹/₂ teaspoon grated orange rind

¹/₄ cup fresh orange juice

3 tablespoons Chinese plum sauce
(see Tip)

1 tablespoon canola or safflower oil

1 teaspoon Dijon mustard

¹/₂ teaspoon minced fresh ginger

¹/₂ teaspoon minced garlic

¹/₈ teaspoon red pepper flakes, or to taste

¹/₈ teaspoon salt, or to taste

To Complete the Recipe

1 medium cucumber, peeled, quartered
lengthwise, seeds removed, and cut into
¹/₄-inch-thick slices (about 1¹/₂ cups);
(see Tip)

¹/₂ cup finely chopped red bell pepper

2 medium scallions, finely chopped

1. Bring a large pot of water to a boil over high heat; add the noodles. When the water returns to a boil, stir occasionally to separate the noodles. Reduce the heat to medium-high and cook for about 6 to 8 minutes, or according to package instructions, until noodles are *al dente*.

184

2. While the noodles are cooking, whisk together the vinaigrette ingredients in a small bowl.

3. When the noodles are done, drain and rinse well in cold water, then drain again.

4. Transfer the noodles to a large bowl. Add the cucumber, bell pepper, and scallions; toss. Add the vinaigrette and toss again. Adjust the seasonings to taste. Chill before serving.

PER SERVING: Cal 184/Prot 6.5g/Carb 32.5g/Fat 3.1g/Chol 0mg/Sod 655mg

ADVANCE PREPARATION   Covered and refrigerated, the vinaigrette will keep for up to 2 days. Cover and refrigerate the completed salad for up to 1 day.

TIPS

- Chinese plum sauce is a thick sweet-and-sour sauce made from plums, apricots, chili peppers, sugar, vinegar, and spices. Look for it in the Asian section of most supermarkets. Store in the refrigerator after opening.

- Many cucumbers are sold with a waxy coating to prolong their shelf life; unfortunately, the wax also seals in pesticides. The only way to remove the wax is by peeling. The unwaxed, elongated European cucumbers (sometimes called hothouse or English cucumbers) are usually the better choice. They are grown hydroponically (in water) without pesticides; and they have an excellent, mild flavor, a more tender texture, and fewer seeds. Store whole cucumbers, unwashed, in a plastic bag in the refrigerator for up to 10 days; once cut, refrigerate them, tightly wrapped, for up to 5 days.

chapter 4

Noodle Soups

HOMEMADE SOUP IS HARD TO BEAT—THERE'S NOTHING
quite so satisfying. And noodle soup, that quintessential
comfort food, is undoubtedly the best of all. From the
familiar ones, like chicken noodle soup and minestrone
soup to elegant soups, like Dilled Shrimp-Pastina Soup
(page 199), they're truly suitable for any occasion. Soups
containing noodles are very popular in Asian cooking, so

don't overlook ramen and udon soups. Here, the proportions are reversed—large helpings of noodles fill the bowls, with the broth and vegetables poured atop. Noisily slurp the noodles if you wish, as Asian custom dictates. That sound signifies utter enjoyment and appreciation.

With the right choice of ingredients, soup no longer needs to simmer for hours. Making soup can be quick and satisfying; in the 15 minutes it takes to prepare these recipes, your kitchen will be filled with inviting aromas.

The foundation for every great pot of soup is the broth; but preparing chicken stock from scratch may not fit into your schedule, as it no longer seems to fit into mine. There is a good alternative. I avoid the chicken-flavored cubes, preferring canned or aseptically fat-free low-sodium chicken broth. Flavorings such as fresh ginger, garlic, soy sauce, dark sesame oil, miso paste, red pepper flakes, tomatoes, and herbs create each soup's distinctive personality. For vegetarian soups, I use an unsalted vegetable stock powder made from dehydrated vegetables or vegetable stock cubes. (Use 1 teaspoon powder or 1 cube per cup of water.) I purchase both products at the health food store; most supermarket varieties are loaded with salt, preservatives, and artificial flavorings. When using ramen noodles, discard the flavor packet packaged with the noodles; plenty of flavor will come from other sources.

Make nothing else for dinner: These soups all can stand on their own as a one-dish meal in a bowl. Asian soups, at their best piping hot, retain their heat in deep noodle bowls, which I accompany with chopsticks for fishing out the solid ingredients, and Chinese soup spoons. The Japanese, rather than using soup spoons, drink their broth straight from the bowl.

Follow these guidelines for noodle soups at their best:

- Thin, brothy soups make the most of narrow strands of pasta and small shapes, such as ramen and soba noodles, pastina, orzo, and alphabets. Chunky soups containing beans, chicken, and larger pieces of vegetables are better suited to thicker and medium-size pasta shapes, such as elbow macaroni and medium pasta shells. Noodles are never added to creamy soups.

- When you want to clear your pantry of partial boxes of dried pasta and noodles, it's a good time to make soup. Soup also provides an easy solution for what to do with odds and ends of vegetables.

- Leftover noodle soups should be covered, refrigerated, and eaten with a couple of days. Noodles absorb liquid, causing the soup to thicken and the noodles to soften. Before reheating, you may need to add more liquid, such as chicken broth, vegetable broth, tomato juice, or water, depending on the recipe. If kept longer than a day or two, some noodles may become mushy.

- These soups can be reheated in individual soup bowls in the microwave or in larger quantities in a pot on top of the stove; be sure to stir frequently.

- I do not recommend freezing soups containing noodles; once thawed, the noodles lose their texture and the soup's flavors deteriorate.

modern
mom's
chicken noodle soup

Makes 4 servings

This restorative chicken noodle soup from my cookbook, The 15-Minute Gourmet: Chicken, *is everybody's favorite. For variety, in place of the noodles, I sometimes substitute cheese-, mushroom-, or chicken-filled tortellini or ravioli to make this a more filling entrée.*

1 tablespoon olive oil

2 carrots, cut into $1/8$-inch-thick slices

$1/4$ cup coarsely chopped onion

1 ($49\frac{1}{2}$-ounce) can fat-free low-sodium chicken broth

8 ounces boneless skinless chicken breast halves, cut into 1-inch-long by $1/2$-inch-wide strips

3 ribs celery, thinly sliced; also shred green tops

2 tablespoons minced fresh flat-leaf parsley

2 teaspoons minced fresh thyme (or $1/2$ teaspoon dried thyme)

$1/4$ teaspoon pepper, or to taste

Dash of salt, or to taste

1 bay leaf (see Tip)

4 ounces wide egg noodles (about 2 cups)

1. Heat the oil in a Dutch oven or soup pot over medium-high heat. Add the carrots and onion; cook, stirring occasionally, for about 2 minutes or until the carrots are crisp-tender and the onion is translucent but not browned. Stir in the chicken broth; cover and increase the heat to high.

2. When the broth comes to a boil, stir in the remaining ingredients. When the liquid returns to a boil, reduce the heat to medium; cover and cook, stirring occasionally, for about 8 to 10 minutes or until the chicken is cooked through and the noodles are tender.

3. Remove the bay leaf. Adjust the seasonings to taste.

PER SERVING: Cal 273/Prot 26.4g/Carb 27.3g/Fat 6.5g/Chol 71mg/Sod 1076mg

ADVANCE PREPARATION   Covered and refrigerated, this soup will keep for up to 2 days.

Variations

- Add other vegetables, such as chunks of plum tomatoes, diced red bell pepper, or frozen peas.

- Substitute dill for the thyme.

- For the noodles, substitute about 8 ounces cheese-, mushroom-, or chicken-filled tortellini or ravioli purchased fresh in the refrigerated section of the super-market. Cook in the soup for 5 to 6 minutes, or according to package instructions. Since these options are more filling than noodles, you may want to reduce the amount of chicken or eliminate it.

> **TIP**
>
> Bay leaf is an aromatic herb that comes from the evergreen bay laurel tree, native to the Mediterranean. Fresh bay leaves are rarely available, but dried bay leaves are found in most supermarkets. Store them in an airtight container in a cool, dark place for up to 6 months. Since overuse will add a bitter flavor, use the leaves in moderation and always remove them before serving the dish.

toasted
noodle
soup

Makes 4 servings

Toasting uncooked noodles gives them a unique flavor. If you have leftover uncooked angel hair pasta or vermicelli; break the strands into 1-inch lengths and substitute for the egg noodles. For a vegetarian version of this soup, substitute vegetable broth for the chicken broth and omit the shrimp. You can substitute beans, such as cannellini beans (use a 19-ounce can, drained and rinsed).

2 tablespoons olive oil

2 cups fine egg noodles (about 4 ounces)

1/2 cup finely chopped onion

1 teaspoon minced garlic

2 (14 1/2-ounce) cans fat-free low-sodium chicken broth

1 (15-ounce) can crushed tomatoes in tomato purée

2 teaspoons minced fresh basil (or 1/2 teaspoon dried basil)

1 teaspoon minced fresh oregano (or 1/2 teaspoon dried oregano)

1/2 teaspoon sugar

1/2 teaspoon pepper, or to taste

1/4 teaspoon salt, or to taste

6 ounces medium shrimp (about 16), shelled and deveined (see Tips)

GARNISH (OPTIONAL)   dollops of plain yogurt or nonfat sour cream, freshly grated Parmesan cheese, minced fresh flat-leaf parsley

1. Heat the oil in a Dutch oven or soup pot over medium-high heat. Add the noodles; cook, stirring constantly, for about 2 minutes or until they are lightly browned. Use a slotted spoon to transfer the noodles to a bowl; set aside.

2. Add the onion and garlic to the remaining oil in the pan; cook, stirring constantly, for about 3 minutes or until fragrant and tender. Stir in the chicken broth, tomatoes and tomato purée, basil, oregano, sugar, pepper, and salt. Cover and increase the heat to high.

3. When the liquid comes to a boil, stir in the noodles and shrimp. Reduce the heat to medium; cover and cook, stirring occasionally, for about 5 minutes or until the noodles are tender and the shrimp are cooked through. Adjust the seasonings to taste.

   PER SERVING: Cal 275/Prot 19.1g/Carb 29.3g/Fat 9g/Chol 93mg/Sod 1330mg

TIPS

- It is not necessary to devein a shrimp for health's sake. It is a matter of personal preference when it comes to small and medium shrimp; the vein of larger shrimp is gritty and removal is recommended. To do so, remove the shell; then, using a sharp knife, make a shallow cut lengthwise down the outermost curve of each shrimp. Remove the sand vein with the point of a knife, and rinse the shrimp under cold running water. Some fish markets sell shrimp that have been shelled; another time-saver ideal for the 15-minute cook is to buy fresh shrimp that have also been deveined.

- Simmer, never boil, shrimp; boiling and overcooking will toughen them. Shrimp are cooked when they just start to turn pink on the outside.

herbed
pasta and
bean soup

Makes 6 servings

The ingredients are waiting right in your pantry to create this hearty meal-in-a-bowl. Vary the recipe by using different beans, such as garbanzo, kidney, Great Northern, or cannellini beans and different pastas, such as medium shells or spaghetti broken into 2-inch lengths.

2 tablespoons olive oil

1/2 green bell pepper, coarsely chopped

1/2 cup coarsely chopped onion

1 teaspoon minced garlic

1 (28-ounce) can diced tomatoes, with juice

1 (14 1/2-ounce) can fat-free low-sodium chicken broth

1/2 teaspoon dried summer savory

1/2 teaspoon dried thyme

1/2 teaspoon pepper, or to taste

1/2 cup elbow macaroni

1 (15-ounce) can pinto beans, drained and rinsed (see Tip)

1/4 cup minced fresh flat-leaf parsley

GARNISH (OPTIONAL)   freshly ground black pepper, freshly grated Parmesan cheese

1. Heat the oil in a Dutch oven or soup pot over medium-high heat. Add the bell pepper, onion, and garlic; cook, stirring occasionally, for about 4 minutes or until tender. Stir in the tomatoes with juice, chicken broth, summer savory, thyme, and pepper; cover and increase the heat to high.

2. When the broth comes to a boil, stir in the macaroni. When the liquid returns to a boil, reduce the heat to medium-high; cover and cook, stirring occasionally, for about 4 to 6 minutes or until the macaroni is *al dente*.

3. Add the beans and parsley; stir gently for about 2 minutes or until heated through. Adjust the seasoning to taste.

PER SERVING: Cal 177/Prot 7g/Carb 25.5g/Fat 5.3g/Chol 0mg/Sod 699mg

ADVANCE PREPARATION   Covered and refrigerated, this soup will keep for up to 2 days.

> ### TIP
>
> Pinto beans, also called red Mexican beans, are grown in the southwestern part of the United States and are commonly used in most Spanish-speaking countries, where they are served with rice or used in soups and stews. They are available both canned and dried in most supermarkets.

Tortellini Soup

tortellini
soup

Makes 4 servings

In their refrigerated and frozen sections, supermarkets carry many varieties of tortellini. My favorite for this recipe is tortellini stuffed with portobello mushrooms and cheese; but more readily available cheese tortellini can be substituted.

2 tablespoons olive oil

1/2 cup finely chopped onion

2 teaspoons minced garlic

2 cups sliced cremini mushrooms (see Tip)

2 (14 1/2-ounce) cans fat-free low-sodium chicken broth

1 (15-ounce) can diced tomatoes, with juice

1 teaspoon Worcestershire sauce

1 tablespoon minced fresh basil (or 1/2 teaspoon dried basil)

1/4 teaspoon pepper, or to taste

8 ounces tortellini

1 tablespoon minced fresh flat-leaf parsley

GARNISH (OPTIONAL)   freshly grated Parmesan cheese

1. Heat the oil in a Dutch oven or soup pot over medium-high heat. Add the onion and garlic; cook, stirring occasionally, for about 2 minutes or until fragrant and almost tender. Add the mushrooms; cook, stirring constantly, about 3 more minutes or until tender. Stir in the chicken broth, tomatoes with juice, Worcestershire sauce, dried basil (if using), and pepper; cover and increase the heat to high.

(continues)

2. When the liquid comes to a boil, stir in the tortellini. Reduce the heat to medium-high; cover and cook, stirring occasionally, for about 5 to 6 minutes, or according to package instructions, just until the tortellini are tender. Stir in the fresh basil (if using) and the parsley. Adjust the seasoning to taste.

PER SERVING (WITH MUSHROOM-FILLED TORTELLINI): Cal 280/Prot 11.7g/Carb 34.3g/Fat 10.7g/Chol 20mg/Sod 750mg

---

TIP

Refrigerate mushrooms for up to 4 days in a paper bag or in a basket so air can circulate around them. Do not wash prior to storage; before using, simply brush with a mushroom brush or wipe with a moist paper towel. If it is necessary to rinse them, do so very quickly; because mushrooms are very absorbent, they should not be allowed to soak in water. Before using, cut off any woody stems and trim the bottoms off tender stems. Mushrooms should be cooked quickly; they are 90 percent water and overcooking results in a mushy texture.

ADVANCE PREPARATION   The vegetable-chicken broth mixture can be cooked up to 2 days in advance; cover and refrigerate. Reheat to cook the tortellini; add the fresh herbs just before serving.

dilled
shrimp-pastina
soup

Makes 4 servings

"Pastina," Italian for "tiny dough," refers to a wide variety of tiny pasta shapes. I like riso, a rice-shaped pasta; but for variety, substitute others, such as shells or alphabets.

1 tablespoon olive oil

2 cups asparagus in 1-inch-long pieces

2 medium leeks, halved lengthwise and cut into $^1/_4$-inch-thick slices (see Tip)

1 (49$^1/_2$-ounce) can fat-free low-sodium chicken broth

$^1/_2$ cup riso pasta (see Tip)

$^1/_4$ cup minced fresh flat-leaf parsley

2 teaspoons snipped fresh dill (or $^3/_4$ teaspoon dried dill)

$^1/_4$ teaspoon pepper, or to taste

$^1/_8$ teaspoon salt, or to taste

8 ounces medium shrimp (about 20), shelled and deveined

1. Heat the oil in a Dutch oven or soup pot over medium-high heat. Add the asparagus and leeks; cook, stirring occasionally, for about 5 minutes or until the asparagus is crisp-tender and the leeks are tender. Stir in the chicken broth; cover and increase the heat to high.

2. When the broth comes to a boil, stir in the riso, parsley, dill, pepper, and salt; cover the pot again. When the liquid returns to a boil, reduce the heat to medium; cook, stirring occasionally, for about 5 minutes or until the riso is *al dente*. Add the shrimp; cover and continue cooking for about 5 more minutes or until the shrimp are cooked through and the riso is tender. Adjust the seasonings to taste.

TIPS

- Leeks, which look like giant scallions, are available year-round in most areas. Select those with crisp bright green leaves and unblemished white bulbs; leeks under 1$^1/_2$ inches in diameter will be the most tender and delicately flavored. Refrigerate them in a plastic bag for up to 5 days. Before using, trim the rootlets and leaf ends. Slit the leeks from top to bottom and wash thoroughly to remove the dirt and sand, which is often trapped between the leaf layers. Use both the white base and the tender portions of the green leaves; discard the tough dark green tops. The flavor is reminiscent of both garlic and onion, although both the taste and fragrance of leeks are milder.

- Riso and orzo, available in most supermarkets, are tiny, rice-shaped pastas; cooking doubles the volume. They can be used as a substitute for rice.

PER SERVING: Cal 286/Prot 23.5g/Carb 35.8g/Fat 5.3g/Chol 87mg/Sod 1117mg

menton soup

Makes 4 servings

This hearty soup, named after a French Riveria town near the Italian border, is a pared-down version of my traditional minestrone recipe that simmers all day, and makes enough to serve a crowd. I rarely follow this recipe exactly, because it is often a destination for odds and ends of vegetables, beans, fresh herbs, and partial packages of pastas. Add a few tablespoons of Basil Pesto (page 100), too, if you like.

2 tablespoons olive oil

$1/2$ cup finely chopped onion

1 teaspoon minced garlic, divided

2 ($14^1/2$-ounce) cans fat-free low-sodium chicken broth

1 ($14^1/2$-ounce) can diced tomatoes, with juice

1 small zucchini, halved lengthwise and cut into $1/4$-inch-thick slices (about 1 cup)

1 cup canned kidney beans, drained and rinsed

1 cup medium ($1/2$- to 1-inch) pasta shells

2 tablespoons tomato paste

$1/4$ cup coarsely chopped fresh flat-leaf parsley

2 tablespoons minced fresh basil (or $1/2$ tablespoon dried basil); (see Tips)

1 tablespoon minced fresh oregano (or $1/2$ tablespoon dried oregano); (see Tips)

$1/4$ teaspoon pepper, or to taste

Dash of salt, or to taste

GARNISH (OPTIONAL)   freshly ground black pepper, freshly grated Parmesan cheese

1. Heat the oil in a Dutch oven or soup pot over medium-high heat. Add the onion and $1/2$ teaspoon of the garlic; cook, stirring constantly, for about 3 minutes or until

fragrant and tender. Stir in the chicken broth and tomatoes with juice. Cover and increase the heat to high.

2. When the liquid comes to a boil, stir in the zucchini, beans, and pasta shells. When the liquid returns to a boil, reduce the heat to medium-high; cover and cook, stirring occasionally, for about 9 to 11 minutes, or according to package instructions, until the shells are tender.

3. While the soup is cooking, stir together the tomato paste, parsley, basil, oregano, pepper, salt, and the remaining $1/2$ teaspoon of garlic in a small bowl. Ladle about $1/4$ cup of the soup liquid into the bowl and stir until smooth; add to the soup. Stir gently until warmed through. Adjust the seasonings to taste.

PER SERVING: Cal 250/Prot 11g/Carb 34.1g/Fat 7.7g/Chol 0mg/Sod 973mg

ADVANCE PREPARATION   Covered and refrigerated, this soup will keep for up to 3 days.

Variations

• Substitute other beans, such as cannellini, pinto, or navy beans, for the kidney beans.

• Substitute spaghetti broken into 2-inch lengths or macaroni for the pasta shells.

TIPS

• Don't wash fresh herbs before storage. Wrap the stem ends with a moist paper towel and refrigerate in a sealed plastic bag. Or place the bunch, stems down, in a glass of water and cover with a plastic bag, securing the bag to the glass with a rubber band; change the water every 2 days. With proper storage, fresh herbs will last for about 1 week; but for the best flavor, use them within a few days. After washing in cool water, dry herbs with paper toweling or in a salad spinner before using.

• Fresh herbs, which come from the leafy part of plants, contain more moisture and therefore are milder than dried herbs. When substituting, use 3 to 4 times more fresh herbs than dried herbs.

salmon
ramen

Makes 4 servings

When buying the salmon for this recipe, I ask the fishmonger to remove the skin from the fillets. If possible, marinate the salmon in teriyaki sauce for at least 30 minutes before broiling. If time does not permit marinating, just brush the sauce on both sides of the salmon; then broil, basting the fillets with the sauce at least once during the cooking period. As you bite into the teriyaki-grilled salmon topped with the ginger and garlic mixture, all of the flavors blend. And personally, I top my bowl with a dash of togarashi (see Tip, page 209) to add a lively touch. This substantial and sensational bowl of soup needs no accompaniment.

4 (3-ounce) pieces salmon fillets, skin removed (see Tip)

$1/4$ cup bottled teriyaki sauce

1 ($49^{1}/_{2}$-ounce) can fat-free low-sodium chicken broth

2 tablespoons low-sodium soy sauce, or to taste, divided

Dash of ground white pepper, or to taste

4 cups coarsely shredded stemmed spinach leaves

3 cups sliced mushrooms

1 cup stemmed snow peas

9 ounces baked ramen noodles

1 teaspoon canola or safflower oil

2 tablespoons minced fresh ginger

2 teaspoons minced garlic

2 medium scallions, finely chopped

GARNISH (OPTIONAL)   togarashi powder, sprigs of fresh cilantro

1. Time permitting, prior to cooking, pour half of the teriyaki sauce into a shallow baking dish. Place the salmon fillets in the sauce; cover with the remaining teriyaki sauce.

Cover and refrigerate for 30 minutes, or for as long as 24 hours, turning the salmon occasionally.

2. When ready to prepare the soup, adjust the oven rack to 4 to 5 inches from heating element; preheat the oven broiler.

3. Pour the chicken broth into a Dutch oven or soup pot; stir in 1 tablespoon of the soy sauce and the pepper. Cover and bring to a boil over high heat.

4. Meanwhile, lightly oil a broiler pan or baking sheet. Remove the salmon fillets from the marinade and place them on the prepared pan; discard the excess marinade. Broil the salmon for about 6 minutes or until cooked through.

> ### TIP
>
> A general rule for cooking fish is to allow 10 minutes per inch of thickness at the thickest part. As fish cooks, its translucent flesh turns opaque. When it is opaque at the thickest part, it is done. Perfectly cooked fish flakes with a fork, another test of doneness.

5. When the chicken broth comes to a boil, reduce the heat to medium, stir in the spinach, mushrooms, and peas; drop in the noodles. Cover and cook for about 3 to 4 minutes or until the vegetables and noodles are *al dente*. As the noodles cook, stir occasionally with a fork to separate. Remove from the heat; adjust the soy sauce and pepper to taste.

6. While the salmon and soup are cooking, heat the oil in a small nonstick skillet over medium-high heat. Add the ginger and garlic; stir constantly for about 2 minutes or until the mixture becomes aromatic. Remove from the heat and stir in the remaining 1 tablespoon of soy sauce.

7. To serve, use tongs to transfer a generous amount of noodles and vegetables to each soup bowl; use a ladle to add the broth. Top each serving with a piece of grilled salmon. Add a dollop of the ginger-garlic mixture and sprinkle with scallions.

PER SERVING: Cal 458/Prot 32.1g/Carb 62.8g/Fat 8.8g/Chol 47mg/Sod 1704mg

Variation

• Rather than broiling the salmon, cook it on an outdoor grill or stovetop grill pan.

Japanese Udon Soup

japanese **udon** soup

Makes 4 servings

I learned to make this soup one memorable winter afternoon when my friend Marcia Nakashima Rogers brought over the ingredients, and I watched as she prepared her Japanese soup recipe—after which we, of course, feasted on the delicious result. This is a modernized and pared-down version of her mom's traditional recipe that was always made with homemade chicken stock.

8 ounces udon noodles

1 (49$\frac{1}{2}$-ounce) can fat-free low-sodium chicken broth

2 tablespoons low-sodium soy sauce, or to taste

16 ounces boneless skinless chicken breast, cut into 1-inch-long by $\frac{1}{2}$-inch-wide strips

2 medium scallions, diagonally cut into $\frac{1}{4}$-inch-thick slices

8 ($\frac{1}{4}$-inch thick) slices kamaboko (see Tip), at room temperature

2 hard-cooked eggs, halved lengthwise and cut into $\frac{1}{4}$-inch-thick slices (see Tip)

1. Bring a large pot of water to a boil over high heat; add the noodles. When the water returns to a boil, stir occasionally to separate the noodles. Cook for about 10 to 12 minutes, or according to package instructions, until noodles are *al dente*.

2. While the noodles are cooking, pour the chicken broth into a Dutch oven or soup pot; stir in the soy sauce. Cover and bring to a boil over high heat. When the broth comes to a boil, stir in the chicken. Reduce the heat to medium; cover and cook, stirring occasionally, for about 8 to 10 minutes or until the chicken is cooked through. Remove from the heat.

(continues)

3. When the noodles are done, drain well; add to the soup after the chicken is done. Stir gently over medium heat until the noodles are heated through. Adjust the seasoning to taste.

4. To serve, use tongs to transfer the noodles and chicken to soup bowls; use a ladle to add the broth. Sprinkle with scallions; then arrange 2 slices of kamaboko and 2 slices of egg on top of each serving.

PER SERVING: Cal 452/Prot 52.6g/Carb 43.4g/Fat 7.6g/Chol 197mg/Sod 2123mg

ADVANCE PREPARATION   Covered and refrigerated, this soup will keep for up to 3 days. If the chicken broth becomes absorbed into the noodles, add more when reheating the soup.

Variations

• Add about 1 teaspoon dark sesame oil or chili oil; stir in with the soy sauce.

• Add 2 cups coarsely shredded Chinese cabbage or stemmed spinach leaves; stir in with the cooked noodles.

• Substitute imitation crabmeat strips for the kamaboko.

• Provide togarashi powder (see Tip, page 209) for your guests to add to the bowls of soup at the table.

TIPS

• Kamaboko is a white, log-shaped cake of steamed fish; food coloring is often used to make the surface pink or red. Ita-kamaboko is shaped into squares or rectangles on small cypress wood planks. Kamaboko is available in the refrigerator or freezer section of Asian markets. Bring the slices to room temperature before using.

• To hard-cook eggs, place them in a single layer in a pan and cover with at least 1 inch of water. Cover and bring the water to a full rolling boil over medium-high heat. Remove the pan from the heat and let the eggs stand in the water, covered, for about 15 minutes. (For larger or smaller eggs, adjust the time up or down by about 3 minutes for each size variation.) Drain off the hot water and immediately cover the eggs with cold water; let stand until the eggs are completely cool. Store in the refrigerator for up to 1 week.

zesty
green vegetable
noodle soup

Makes 4 servings

This simple soup is one of my standbys for a busy weeknight when appetites are hearty but time doesn't permit standing over the stove for long.

1 tablespoon canola or safflower oil

4 cups coarsely shredded stemmed spinach leaves

4 cups finely shredded Chinese cabbage (see Tip)

2 medium scallions, finely chopped

2 teaspoons minced fresh ginger

1 teaspoon minced garlic

1 ($49^{1}/_{2}$-ounce) can fat-free low-sodium chicken broth

1 tablespoon low-sodium soy sauce, or to taste

1 teaspoon chili paste with garlic, or to taste

4 ounces thin Chinese wheat-flour noodles

> **TIP**
>
> Chinese cabbage, also called Napa cabbage, can be recognized by its white, solid oblong heads with crinkly, thick-veined, pale green leaves. Unlike head cabbage, Chinese cabbage is mild and delicate. It can be used raw and becomes tender when stir-fried, sautéed, baked, or braised. In most supermarkets, it is available year-round. Refrigerated tightly wrapped, it will keep for up to 3 days.

1. Heat the oil in Dutch oven or soup pot over medium-high heat. Add the spinach, cabbage, scallions, ginger, and garlic; cook, stirring constantly, for about 2 minutes or until the spinach and cabbage are wilted.

2. Stir in the chicken broth, soy sauce, and chili paste; cover and increase heat to high.

3. When the broth comes to a boil, add the noodles. When the water returns to a boil, reduce the heat to medium-high and cook, stirring occasionally, for about 3 to 5 minutes or until the noodles are tender. As the noodles cook, stir occasionally with a fork to separate. Adjust the seasonings to taste.

4. To serve, use tongs to transfer the noodles and vegetables to soup bowls; use a ladle to add the broth.

PER SERVING: Cal 199/Prot 11.2g/Carb 29.2g/Fat 4.2g/Chol 0mg/Sod 1496mg

asian
noodle soup
with **spinach and corn**

Makes 4 servings

This Asian soup was inspired by a satisfying lunch my son and I enjoyed in a charming San Francisco noodle restaurant that was recommended by insiders. The flavor is at its best when fresh corn is available; but in the winter, frozen corn will do. I provide togarashi powder or red pepper flakes at the table for guests to add just the right amount of hotness each prefers.

1 (49½-ounce) can fat-free low-sodium chicken broth

2 tablespoons low-sodium soy sauce

Dash of ground white pepper, or to taste

6 ounces baked ramen noodles

2 cups fresh corn; cut from about 4 ears (see Tip) or frozen corn, thawed

12 cups coarsely shredded stemmed spinach leaves

Dash of red pepper flakes or togarashi powder (see Tip), or to taste

4 teaspoons butter

1. Pour the chicken broth into a Dutch oven or soup pot; stir in the soy sauce and pepper. Cover and bring to a boil over high heat. Stir in the fresh corn (if using) and drop in the noodles. Reduce the heat to medium-high; cover and cook for about 2 to 3 minutes or until the noodles are *al dente*. As the noodles cook, stir occasionally with a fork to separate.

2. Reduce the heat to medium. Add the thawed frozen corn (if using), spinach, and the red pepper flakes or togarashi; cover and cook, stirring occasionally, for about 1 minute or until the spinach is wilted and the noodles are tender. Adjust the seasonings to taste.

3. To serve, use tongs to transfer generous amounts of noodles, spinach, and corn to 4 soup bowls; use a ladle to add the broth. Top each steaming bowl of soup with a teaspoon-size slice of butter.

PER SERVING: Cal 356/Prot 16.6g/Carb 59.7g/Fat 5.6g/Chol 10mg/Sod 1572mg

Variation

• Substitute lo mein noodles for the ramen noodles.

TIPS

• Because the sugar immediately begins to convert to starch when corn is picked, it is best to buy fresh corn for immediate use. To make the most of fresh corn's natural sweetness, refrigerate it for no more than 1 day before using.

• Togarashi is a small, hot, red Japanese chili; it is available in several dried forms, rounds, flakes and powder. You'll find several varieties in Asian stores. "Ichimi" togarashi contains only the chili powder; "nanomi" togarshi contains the chili powder plus additional ingredients, such as sesame seeds, seaweed, and orange peel. (Either can be used in my recipes calling for togarashi.)

egg drop
noodle
soup

Makes 4 servings

I've simplified this classic in Chinese cooking for speedy preparation; and by adding lots of noodles, it becomes a substantial meal.

1 (49^1/$_2$-ounce) can fat-free low-sodium chicken broth

2 tablespoons low-sodium soy sauce

2 ounces oyster mushroom caps, cut into ^{1}/$_2$-inch-wide strips (about 1 cup); (see Tip)

^{1}/$_2$ cup red bell pepper in 1^1/$_2$-inch long by ^{1}/$_8$-inch wide strips

1 medium carrot, coarsely shredded

^{1}/$_2$ cup frozen baby peas, thawed

1 medium scallion, minced

1 teaspoon minced garlic

Dash of ground white pepper, or to taste

3 ounces baked ramen noodles

2 eggs, lightly beaten

1 teaspoon dark sesame oil, or to taste

GARNISH   toasted sesame seeds, thin scallion slices

1. Pour the chicken stock into a Dutch oven or soup pot; stir in the soy sauce. Cover and bring to a boil over high heat. Stir in the mushrooms, bell pepper, carrot, peas, scallion, garlic, pepper, and noodles. Cover and cook for about 2 to 3 minutes or until the vegetables and noodles are nearly tender. As the noodles cook, stir occasionally with a fork to separate.

2. Reduce the heat to medium. Add the eggs slowly, pouring in a very thin stream while stirring briskly and constantly. Continue stirring for about 2 minutes or until the eggs cook and form shreds. Stir in the sesame oil. Adjust the seasonings to taste.

PER SERVING: Cal 192/Prot 11.9g/Carb 26.2g/Fat 4.4g/Chol 107mg/Sod 1041mg

ADVANCE PREPARATION   The stock and vegetables can be cooked up to 1 day in advance; cover and refrigerate. Reheat to cook the noodles and eggs; add the sesame oil just before serving.

Variations

- Substitute vegetable stock for the chicken stock.

- Substitute $1/2$ cup cholesterol-free egg substitute for the eggs.

> **TIP**
>
> Oyster mushrooms are graceful, fluted mushrooms that vary in color from pale gray to dark brownish-gray. The flavor is robust and slightly peppery but becomes much milder when cooked. Oyster mushrooms are available in some markets year-round, particularly in specialty produce and Asian markets. Look for young mushrooms, $1^1/2$ inches or less in diameter; remove the tough part of the stems before cooking.

miso soup
with ramen
noodles

Makes 6 servings

Dark miso paste has the consistency of peanut butter but smells and tastes like soy sauce. Only a small amount turns a blah stock into a gourmet's dream; this rich flavor is the kind you usually get only from lengthy cooking times. The secret behind the seductive hint of sweetness is apple juice.

1 (49$\frac{1}{2}$-ounce) can fat-free low-sodium chicken broth

2 tablespoons dark miso paste (see Tip)

2 tablespoons cornstarch

$\frac{1}{4}$ cup apple juice

1 carrot, finely shredded

$\frac{1}{8}$ teaspoon red pepper flakes, or to taste

6 ounces baked ramen noodles

12 ounces silken extra-firm tofu, cut into $\frac{1}{2}$-inch cubes (about 2 cups)

GARNISH (OPTIONAL)   toasted sesame seeds, minced scallions, shredded nori or wakame (see Tips)

1. Stir together $\frac{1}{4}$ cup of the chicken broth and the miso paste in a small bowl until smooth. Pour into a Dutch oven or soup pot. Stir in the remaining chicken broth.

2. In a small bowl, stir together the cornstarch and apple juice until smooth; add to the soup pot. Stir in the carrot and red pepper flakes. Stir the mixture constantly over medium-high heat for about 3 minutes or until it is slightly thickened and partially clear. Increase the heat to high.

3. When the broth nearly comes to a boil (it's best not to boil cornstarch mixtures or miso), drop in the noodles. Reduce the heat to medium-high; cover and cook for about 2 to 3 minutes or until the noodles are *al dente*. As the noodles cook, stir occasionally with a fork to separate.

4. Reduce the heat to low; gently stir in the tofu. Heat for about 2 minutes or until it is warmed through. Adjust the seasoning to taste.

PER SERVING: Cal 139/Prot 10.3g/Carb 19.1g/Fat 2.4g/Chol 0mg/Sod 926mg

Variations

• For a hint of the sea, add a 3-inch piece of kombu seaweed (see Tip) to the chicken broth; cover and boil for about 10 minutes. Remove the seaweed and proceed with the recipe.

• When adding the carrot, also add 1 cup thinly sliced mushrooms.

TIPS

• Miso, or fermented soybean paste, is a basic flavoring in Japanese cooking. It comes in a wide variety of colors, ranging from light yellow to a dark red-brown, with a corresponding intensity of flavor. All of the types are made from soybeans and a whole grain; the mixture is then aged in cedar vats for 1 month to 3 years. Miso is found in Japanese markets and health food stores. Refrigerated in an airtight container, it will keep for up to 2 months; or it can be frozen for up to 4 months.

• Nori are paper-thin, dark green sheets of seaweed that are generally used for wrapping sushi. When cut into thin strips, it serves as a seasoning or garnish. Nori is available in Asian markets and in the gourmet section of some supermarkets. It can be purchased pretoasted; if untoasted, it should be held briefly over a flame to crisp the texture and brighten its color before using. Store in a tightly sealed package at room temperature away from light, heat, and most importantly from moisture.

• Wakame is a dark green edible seaweed that is used like a vegetable in soups, simmered dishes, and salads. The browner varieties are more strongly flavored. Wakame is available both in fresh and dried forms in most Asian markets.

• Kombu seaweed, or kelp, is a long dark brown or grayish-black seaweed. After harvesting, it is sun-dried and folded into sheets. When cooked in soup stock, it enhances the flavor. Once cooked, the kombu can be removed and discarded. Or, if you like, remove the rib, chop the leaf, and add it to the soup. Kombu is found in Asian markets and health food stores. Store kombu in a cool, dry place for up to 6 months.

orange
soba noodle
soup

Makes 4 servings

This soup has been a perennial favorite of my cooking-class students. The red pepper flakes and citrus aroma are guaranteed to stimulate your senses; adjust the amount to suit your taste.

1 (49$^1/_2$-ounce) can fat-free low-sodium chicken broth

8 ounces boneless skinless chicken breast halves, cut into 1-inch-long by $^1/_2$-inch-wide strips

8 ounces soba noodles

$^1/_2$ cup coarsely shredded carrot

2 medium scallions, finely chopped (see Tip)

1 tablespoon low-sodium soy sauce

1 teaspoon minced garlic

$^1/_2$ teaspoon red pepper flakes, or to taste

$^1/_8$ teaspoon ground white pepper, or to taste

1 teaspoon orange zest

$^1/_4$ cup fresh orange juice

1 teaspoon dark sesame oil, or to taste

GARNISH   chopped scallions and toasted sesame seeds

1. Pour the chicken broth into a Dutch oven or soup pot; cover and bring to a boil over high heat.

2. Stir in the chicken, noodles, carrot, scallions, soy sauce, garlic, red pepper flakes, and white pepper. When the broth returns to a boil, reduce the heat to medium; cover and cook, stirring occasionally, for about 8 to 10 minutes or until the chicken is cooked through and the noodles are tender.

3. Stir in the remaining ingredients. Adjust the seasonings to taste.

4. To serve, use tongs to fill large soup bowls with the cooked noodles and chicken; use a ladle to add the broth and vegetables.

PER SERVING: Cal 342/Prot 27.4g/Carb 51.5g/Fat 2.9g/Chol 44mg/Sod 1144mg

ADVANCE PREPARATION   Covered and refrigerated, this soup will keep for up to 1 day.

Variations

- When adding the carrot, add other vegetables (up to 2 cups) such as mushrooms, bok choy (both sliced ribs and shredded greens), peas, or stemmed snow peas.

- Just before serving, stir in minced fresh cilantro.

TIP

Scallions, also called green onions or spring onions, come from the thinnings of immature onion bulbs as well as certain kinds of onions that produce long, thin stems. The leaves should be bright green and firm; the white bottoms should be firm, unblemished, and free of soil. Both parts can be used in recipes calling for scallions. The size varies from very slender to large and thick; as a rule, the more slender the bottoms, the sweeter the flavor. Store scallions for up to 1 week, wrapped in a plastic bag, in the vegetable crisper section of the refrigerator.

index

Page numbers in *italics* refer to illustrations.